The poetry of
Dante Gabriel Rossetti:
modes of self-expression

The poetry of
Dante Gabriel Rossetti:
modes of self-expression

JOAN REES

CAMBRIDGE UNIVERSITY PRESS

CAMBRIDGE

LONDON   NEW YORK   NEW ROCHELLE
MELBOURNE   SYDNEY

Published by the Press Syndicate of the University of Cambridge
The Pitt Building, Trumpington Street, Cambridge CB2 IRP
32 East 57th Street, New York, NY 10022, USA
296 Beaconsfield Parade, Middle Park, Melbourne 3206, Australia

© Cambridge University Press 1981

First published 1981

Printed in Great Britain by The Anchor Press Ltd
and bound by Wm Brendon & Son Ltd
both of Tiptree, Essex

British Library Cataloguing in Publication Data

Rees, Joan
The poetry of Dante Gabriel Rossetti.
1. Rossetti, Dante Gabriel – Criticism and interpretation
I. Title
821'.8   PR5247   80–40904

ISBN 0 521 23537 5

Contents

Note

Rossetti's life has been copiously documented. His brother, William Michael, wrote extensively about him and the list of subsequent biographies has recently been extended by the addition of *D. G. Rossetti: An Alien Victorian* by B. and J. Dobbs (London, 1977). The amount of biographical work far outstrips the attention given to the scope and nature of Rossetti's achievement as a poet, and since so much material on the life is available, biographical matters have been given only minimal attention in this book.

The following abbreviations will be used:

Letters of Dante Gabriel Rossetti, edited by Oswald Doughty and J. R. Wahl, 4 volumes, Oxford, 1965–7, referred to as *Letters*.

D. G. Rossetti's Collected Works, edited by W. M. Rossetti, 2 volumes, London, 1886, referred to as *Works*.

The Paintings and Drawings of Dante Gabriel Rossetti. A Catalogue Raisonné, by Virginia Surtees, referred to as Surtees, followed by the catalogue number of the work in question.

Introduction
Poets and Pre-Raphaelites

FOUR Pre-Raphaelite anthologies have been published in recent years,[1] all addressing themselves to the problem of defining what the term Pre-Raphaelite may signify in relation to poetry since, as a descriptive label applied to literature, it is in itself plainly meaningless. The most useful of their comments are the most general for, as W. E. Fredeman observes:

No single catalogue of external characteristics can convey the complexity of the Pre-Raphaelite aesthetic or carry the burden of the term's definition.[2]

He runs through such a catalogue to illustrate his point:

a realism derived from the literal observation and truthful rendering of nature; a preoccupation with external detail for its own sake; the reintroduction of vivid colouration into painting; a predisposition to medieval themes and subjects, with overtones of an 'Early Christian' ethic; artistic sincerity in the treatment of subjects and emotions; the use of obvious literary sources as the inspiration for art

– the catalogue applies, with obvious modifications, to both poetry and painting but Fredeman dismisses it and others like it as 'inevitably misleading'.

[1] *The Pre-Raphaelite Poem*, edited by James D. Merritt (New York, 1966), *The Pre-Raphaelites*, edited by Jerome H. Buckley (New York, 1968), *The Pre-Raphaelites and their Circle*, edited by Cecil Y. Lang (Boston, 1968) and, most recently, *Pre-Raphaelite Writing*, edited by Derek Stanford (London, 1973).
[2] In his contribution on 'The Pre-Raphaelites' in *The Victorian Poets: A Guide to Research*, edited by Frederic E. Faverty, 2nd edition, (Cambridge, Mass., 1968).

A reader who takes such lists seriously as a guide to the poetry is liable to conclude at best that the Pre-Raphaelite programme was arbitrary and he may well find it merely silly. The need, evidently, is for some grasp of what lies behind the various superficial characteristics. Fredeman writes that Pre-Raphaelitism in art and literature 'was a revolt against the rules of the academicians and a re-assertion of faith in the truth of the creative expression of the individual artist as opposed to the stereotyped and conventionalised expression of pseudo-"classical" art'.[1] The phrasing of this is biased towards painting but it clears some ground for the poetry also. Lang takes us further when he writes that if Pre-Raphaelitism is to be used as a critical term for poetry 'it has to mean some-thing like "visualised poetry of fantasy" or "fantasy crossed with realism" '. This comment points valuably to a central area in the imaginative experience of Pre-Raphaelite poetry. Buckley is also helpful. Beneath divergencies of method and paradoxes and inconsisten-cies of theory, he writes, there is in Pre-Raphaelite painting and poetry 'a certain community of spirit':

Each of the painters and poets, in his own way or in more than one way, raised his protest against the comfortable assumptions of a matter-of-fact world. Each sought to recover the sense of wonder and mystery, the dream beyond the commonplaces of an order increasingly devoted to the mechanization of human life. Each strove to make his art the vehicle of a fresh intuition.

With these comments in mind it is possible to make some sense of the impulses which lie behind 'heavy' use of detail, mystery, medievalism and the rest. As is commonly recognised and as the Pre-Raphaelites were the first to acknowledge, Pre-Raphaelitism was a develop-ment out of the Romantic movement of the earlier years of the century. Holman Hunt bought a copy of Keats's then little-known poems for fourpence one day in 1848

[1] W. E. Fredeman, *Pre-Raphaelitism, A Bibliocritical Study* (Cambridge Mass, 1965), p. 2.

and carried it back to be the delight and inspiration of his companions. In 1847 Rossetti acquired for ten shillings from a British Museum attendant a manuscript book of Blake's (o tempora . . .) and was among the first to recognise his genius. Later he worked hard as collaborator in Gilchrist's edition and he preached Blake's merits as poet and painter all his life. The five English poets for whom he wrote sonnets (published in 1881) were all Romantics, Chatterton, Blake, Coleridge, Keats and Shelley. 'The excellence of every art is its intensity', Keats wrote, and: 'What the imagination seizes as Beauty must be truth . . . I have never yet been able to perceive how any thing can be known for truth by consequitive reasoning . . .'[1] The two remarks might well be taken as the distinguishing notes of that 'community of spirit' which Buckley finds among the Pre-Raphaelites, for intensity, whether in the painter's delineation of pregnant moments or Rossetti's concentrated attempts to articulate his inner life in verse, is a hallmark of Pre-Raphaelitism. As for the relation between truth perceived by the imagination and truth arrived at by consecutive reasoning, Pre-Raphaelitism takes its stand unequivocally by the imagination. Buckley again writes helpfully: '. . . the Pre-Raphaelites achieved their difference by repudiating the world that was too much with their contemporaries. To the mechanical standardisation of parts they opposed the fresh apprehension of detail. To the quantitative measurement of large impersonal things, they preferred the qualitative analysis of their own intense perceptions.'

The Pre-Raphaelite Brotherhood as it was formed in 1848 was only a group of boys, as Rossetti himself in later life dismissively described it, rebelling in immature arrogance against the teaching of their masters. But they were very talented boys and one of them was brilliant.

[1] Letters to George and Thomas Keats, 21 December 1817, and to Benjamin Bailey, 22 November 1817.

They were able to inject into an increasingly mechanistic society a reminder of other values where analysis and calculation played no part and where 'utility' whether in its physical or moral applications was of no concern. Their art was not the only channel through which the quality of nineteenth-century life was being attacked, though the attacking forces were sometimes reluctant to recognise their allies. In particular, those who waged their campaign on social and political fronts did not necessarily enjoy having their own conventional prejudices disturbed in the field of art. Dickens, for example, reacted with notorious virulence to Millais' attempt to imagine intensely the life of Christ in the house of His parents. The Pre-Raphaelite Brotherhood as such had only a short span of existence but Pre-Raphaelitism as a call for a fresh vision, a challenge to orthodoxies and assumptions and a resistance to the depersonalising pressures of the industrial world, had a continuing and vigorous life throughout the century. It lingers yet and our own even more commercialised society makes, ironically enough, a good thing out of Pre-Raphaelite posters and calendars and even shopping bags to take to the supermarket.

Manifestations of Pre-Raphaelitism at the end of the nineteenth century were many and various. One of the best known in its own day and for years afterwards and one of the least known now is Watts-Dunton's novel *Aylwin*. Watts-Dunton was a solicitor, a poet and a critic. He is best remembered now for his care (some would say his abuse) of Swinburne in his later years but he was also an intimate friend of Rossetti's and admired him greatly. One of the most evocative passages in Max Beerbohm's splendid and witty essay 'No. 2, The Pines', recounting a visit to the Swinburne–Watts-Dunton ménage, describes the paintings of Rossetti women looming 'vivid and vital' on the walls. Watts-Dunton composed several accounts of Rossetti and *Aylwin* contains one of them, fictionalised and romanticised. More important in relation to the novel's Pre-Raphaelite connections, however, is the sub-title *The Renascence of Wonder*, for *Aylwin* bears only too abundant witness to the late Victorian yearning for some escape from a mechanistic universe. Celtic superstition, gypsy second sight, gnostic lore, spiritualism – a whole gamut of anti-rational beliefs and practices is run through in the novel. At the centre of it are painters, D'Arcy (Rossetti) amongst them, who are open to the mystery of things and refuse to shut their minds to possibilities which science counts impossible. 'We have our philosophical persons, to make modern and familiar, things supernatural and causeless', says Lafeu in Shakespeare's *All's Well that Ends Well*. 'Hence is it that we make trifles of terrors, ensconcing ourselves into seeming knowledge when we should submit ourselves to an unknown fear.' Watts-Dunton says the same, rather less cogently. His message, his case for a renascence of wonder, is a late version of romanticism and he traces its lineage consciously and pointedly through the Pre-Raphaelites. *Aylwin* was an outstanding best-seller. It went through twenty-six editions by the time of Watts-Dunton's death in 1914 and was reprinted throughout the 1920s. It is scarcely heard of now.

An outgrowth from Pre-Raphaelitism which is more publicised nowadays was the aesthetic movement of later years of the century. As with Pre-Raphaelitism, argument has raged and still rages over definitions and implications. The aesthetes claimed their inheritance from Rossetti and there can be no doubt of his great influence upon them but the connection has not done much good to his reputation or to that of the Pre-Raphaelites in general. There is no reason to argue the pros and cons of aestheticism here but a few observations are relevant. In so far as aestheticism was a decadent movement they were Pre-Raphaelite ideas which were in decay. The sense of beauty may easily become a self-inclosed cult, belief in the truth of the imagination may create what Oscar Wilde called 'a separate realm', liable to impoverishment by lack of contact with the general life, and intensity may become a feverish pursuit of sensation – any sensation – for its own sake. Aestheticism bred the Rhymers' Club of the 1890s and a generation of writers whose tragic non-fulfilment Yeats observed when he was young. They incurred ridicule and opprobrium but in fact the voice of moral outrage against contemporary romanticism had been making itself heard for some time. Swinburne's *Poems and Ballads* of 1866 defied moral orthodoxies and conventional assumptions much more flagrantly than previous Pre-Raphaelite work had done and when Rossetti published his own first volume four years later he came in for a discharge of accumulated animosity. Yet Rossetti sought to tone down Swinburne's stridencies and he himself never subscribed to the immoralist tendencies of later aestheticism. Art for art's sake is a formula of divers possible meanings, some of which Rossetti would have endorsed, but the idea that art should have reference to itself alone he did not accept. As he grew older he became more and more seriously convinced that he had something to say about his life's experience which he was impelled to record not for his own relief simply, but that other men might read and note.

II

The extent to which Pre-Raphaelitism is to be seen in the context of nineteenth-century developments of romanticism has been briefly indicated. The Pre-Raphaelites played a vital and central role as breachers of artistic convention on the one side and as champions of fidelity to a new 'truth' on the other. What was involved in Pre-Raphaelite 'truth' now needs more discussion. In 1851 Ruskin put the weight of his already considerable reputation behind the Pre-Raphaelite Brotherhood painters in two famous letters to *The Times* and in the same year he wrote in his essay, *Pre-Raphaelitism*, that painters should 'be truthful. It is more difficult and worthy of the greatest men's greatest effort, to render, as it should be rendered, the simplest of the natural features of the earth.' When, six years earlier, he had been to Italy, another aspect of 'truth' had made a great impression on him. In a letter to his father in 1845 he wrote of the frescoes he had seen in Pisa: 'the Campo Santo is the thing. I never believed the Patriarchal history before, but I do now, for I have seen it . . . Abraham and Adam, and Cain, Rachel and Rebekah, all are there, real, visible, created, substantial, such as they were, as they must have been . . . Abraham sits *close* to you.'[1] The two qualities celebrated by Ruskin, fidelity to natural detail and dramatic immediacy in the treatment of a scene, comprise a great deal of what the Pre-Raphaelites meant by 'truth'. But here, to complicate the issue, comes in Lang's observation that something which is not realism – he calls it 'fantasy' but that is not altogether a satisfactory word – is crossed with realism in Pre-Raphaelite poetry. Buckley is similarly thinking of ambiguities in Pre-Raphaelite 'realism' when he writes of the painting that in the best work of Millais and Hunt, 'their realism becomes surrealistic, and it is not surprising that Salvador Dali could see a kinship between their painting and his own'.

Useful assistance in pinpointing the issues involved in this matter comes from the younger Rossetti brother, William Michael. In his capacity as deeply conscientious secretary to the Brotherhood, William Michael wrote a sonnet for the cover of *The Germ*, the Pre-Raphaelite Brotherhood magazine which, started in January 1850, ran to four monthly numbers and then collapsed. Its

---

[1] Quoted by Richard L. Stein, *The Ritual of Interpretation* (Cambridge, Mass. and London, 1975), p. 122.

propagative qualities, however, far outlived its short career. The sub-title, evolved by Dante Gabriel, was 'Thoughts towards Nature in Poetry, Literature and Art' and William's sonnet tries to describe what it is that the small band of contributors are getting at. 'When whoso merely hath a little thought', he begins:

> Will plainly think the thought which is in him, –
> Not imaging another's bright or dim,
> Not mangling with new words what others taught . . .

When he has done this and conveyed it in 'that very speech the matter brought', then truth has been spoken and

> . . . be the theme a point or the whole earth,
> Truth is a circle, perfect great or small.

Truth, then, is looking freshly at a subject and recording scrupulously and accurately what one sees; but, although this metaphor offers itself readily by way of paraphrase, it is in fact a striking feature of the sonnet that William Rossetti writes entirely in terms of thinking rather than seeing. The same emphasis occurs in *The Germ*'s sub-title, '*Thoughts* towards Nature . . .' This title and William Michael's sonnet might almost lead an unprepared reader to expect a volume of metaphysical essays. Philosophical and psychological concepts must always be involved in any programme which invokes words like 'truth' and 'nature' and the Rossetti brothers were far too intelligent to be unaware of this. They were not philosophers but neither did they think that to follow Nature was a simple act of transcription and they understood that the 'truth' they sought was not a given fact but something relative to the individual mind. Two of Dante Gabriel's poems illustrate neatly the limits of 'realism' as he practised it. 'My Sister's Sleep' and 'The Bride's Prelude' both contain descriptions of domestic interiors with close attention to small detail but their effect has nothing in common with the work of the great Dutch painters. In 'My Sister's Sleep' physical observation is suffused with a sense of

spiritual mystery and in 'The Bride's Prelude' the sights
and sounds of a summer day enter an atmosphere
charged with guilt and passion and derive an extra-
normal, 'surreal', intensity from it. Rossetti's observation
turned more and more inward as years went by and in the
sonnet sequence *The House of Life* (Swinburne thought
the image was again a domestic one, with the sonnet
stanzas as rooms – Italian *stanze*) all his powers of observation are brought into the service of recording not the
outer but the inner consciousness.

'Thought', like 'fantasy', may not be the best word to
indicate what is blended with Pre-Raphaelite 'realism',
though both words are applicable at different times and
in different proportions and each points to an activity in
the mind of poet or painter. What the quality and resources
of this mind are will obviously determine the nature of
the results. William Michael Rossetti is again useful as an
illuminator. In September 1849 he began work on a
poem which was eventually published under the title
'Mrs Holmes Grey'. W. E. Fredeman has described it as
a key poem of the Pre-Raphaelite movement and draws
attention to its 'Pre-Raphaelite penchant for ultra-
realism in the depiction of detail'.[1] There is certainly no
element of fantasy in it. The poem tells the story of a wife
who becomes possessed by a revived and uncontrollable
passion for a man she has known before her marriage and
whom she now meets again. She pursues the man to his
own home and importunes him with her passion.
Eventually he tells her finally and firmly that he is unable
to respond and that she must return to her husband,
whereupon she falls dead at his feet. The story is a sensational one but it is told with unrelieved and deliberate
flatness. Rossetti goes so far, indeed, as to recount the

[1] 'A Key Poem of the Pre-Raphaelite Movement: William Michael
Rossetti's "Mrs Holmes Grey"', *Nineteenth Century Perspectives: Essays
in Honour of Lionel Stevenson*, edited by Clyde de la Ryals (Durham, N.C.,
1974), pp. 149–59.

climactic events in the form of a newspaper report of the coroner's inquest on Mrs Grey's death. The poem represents one aspect of Pre-Raphaelite 'truth' and 'realism', a literal account, so it would seem, of an episode, verse denying itself its prerogatives of rhetoric, rhythm and imagery and depending on the steady, un-wavering gaze which defines the events and lets them stand out with sharp clarity. William Rossetti is rejecting the literary equivalent of the varnish which gave a dark patina to the (then uncleaned) paintings of the Old Masters and aiming at something like the clear bold colouring of early Italian painters; but there is more to it than that. The poem is prefaced by an epigraph from Poe: 'Perverseness is one of the primitive impulses of the human heart; one of the indivisible primary faculties or sentiments which give direction to the character of man.' The quotation and its source leave no doubt that William Rossetti's primary inspiration in the composition of the poem was interest in a psychological situation – more accurately, in *two* psychological situations, for the husband's state of mind after the death is as curious as the wife's before it. It follows that to concentrate on the remorseless factuality employed in the poem is to give a much less than adequate account of 'Mrs Holmes Grey' and also of its significance in relation to Pre-Raphaelite poetry in general. To begin with, it should be stressed that the method is being applied to material which is in itself very strange indeed and, beyond that, the full scope of the experiment needs to be recognised. William Michael declared that 'The informing idea of the poem was to apply to verse-writing the same principle of strict actuality and probability of detail which the Pre-Raphael-ites upheld in their pictures',[1] but he explains further, in

---

[1] *Family Letters of Dante Gabriel Rossetti with a Memoir*, edited by W. M. Rossetti, 1895, ii, p. 63. The poem has recently been edited by W. E. Fredeman and is printed in *The P.R.B. Journal* edited by Fredeman (Oxford, 1975).

an accompanying note to the poem, that in approaching 'nearer to the actualities of dialogue and narration than had ever yet been done', he had by no means intended to forfeit 'the poetic, dramatic, or even tragic tone and impression'. The technique employed, in other words, is being tried as a means of achieving certain results, in this instance to allow of a sharp, unimpeded realisation of emotional disorders of a highly dramatic kind. The ideas behind the experiment are not unlike Wordsworth's in the *Lyrical Ballads*, which he expounded in the famous Preface, and, as a doctrinaire poem, the product of thought and theory, 'Mrs Holmes Grey' is of considerable interest. But the 'certain colouring of imagination' on which Wordsworth relied is not of deep enough dye in William Rossetti's work and as a Pre-Raphaelite poem it indicates rather what the greater talents do not do rather than what they do. There is a good deal of 'thought' mixed with William Michael's 'realism' and it relates in large part to an interest in the psychological aspects of 'truth' which he shared with his brother but the methods adopted were too limited for Dante Gabriel. His mind was stored with rarer and richer furnishings than could be admitted through the narrow door which 'Mrs Holmes Grey' unlocked. Interest in the psychology of love produced when he wrote, not a police court case, but Sister Helen burning the wax effigy of her false lover, and the influence of Poe led directly to 'The Blessed Damozel'. More often than not in his work psychological interest produces 'fantastic' scenes rather than authentic scenes of contemporary life but they are none the less 'true' since they give faithful images of what is perceived within consciousness itself. We have to give up separating 'thought' and 'fantasy' and 'realism' when we speak of the elder Rossetti's best and most characteristic work and talk instead of his imaginative world, a whole in which these parts still function but are blended so that they lose their separate natures and compose something which is different from any.

Lists of Pre-Raphaelite features are ineffective as indicators of what lay at the root of the movement. The paradox that Pre-Raphaelite pursuit of 'nature' and 'truth' leads to a poetry in which realism is blended with something not realistic at all, whether it be fantasy, superstition, surrealism, or an archaising fancy is similarly unproductive of a neat conclusion. Underlying the catalogues of Pre-Raphaelite characteristics is the romantic spirit of rebellion against a mechanistic society. Underlying the paradox is a related part of the inheritance from Romanticism, the urge towards expression of the self. Buckley's comment that each of the Pre-Raphaelites 'strove to make his art the vehicle of a fresh intuition' makes an important point and 'Mrs Holmes Grey' fails as a Pre-Raphaelite poem precisely because it confines itself to too much objectivity. Pre-Raphaelitism provided a release and a means of expression for an individual response to experience. So many poets and painters, so many personalities, and the impossibility, therefore, of codifying them, in spite of 'community of spirit', into a group subscribing to the same laws and practices. Pre-Raphaelitism, by its deliberate divergence from the currents of contemporary belief and opinion, encouraged individuals to express their own personal selves and Pre-Raphaelite techniques and attitudes, used in whatever proportions individuals found suitable, offered them a means of doing it. Upon the Middle Ages they could project whatever they yearned for and found missing in their own lives, through colour they could provide the richness that industrial landscapes were destroying, through the use of closely observed detail they could sharpen their senses and sensibilities . . . and so on.

There were powerful forces working against them. The French Revolution with all its implications and consequences had helped first and second generation Romantics to define themselves but the strong development of the notion of social responsibility in the mid-nineteenth century discouraged the frank expression of individual sensibility. Tennyson struggled *not* to cultivate those aspects of his temperament which led Harold Nicolson to call him a 'black unhappy mystic of the Lincolnshire wolds'. He trained himself to embrace instead the role of 'seer-in-ordinary' to the Victorian household (Humbert Wolfe's phrase). Arnold gave up the writing of poetry which expressed his personal despair in 'an age wanting in moral grandeur . . . and an age of spiritual discomfort'[1] and took up the task of reforming the times in prose. Browning created his Men and Women and Dramatis Personae through whose mouths he might say what he wished without an unacceptable degree of self-exposure but, even so, his style and subjects were objectionably eccentric in many eyes.[2] The Pre-Raphaelite poets went their own way, offering, implicitly if not avowedly, an alternative culture to the official one, deriving some strength from their position but also considerably weakened by it. Though Swinburne in one way and Morris in another did, Rossetti did not wish to challenge society but could manage no more than an uneasy relationship with it which contributed to his breakdown and neurotic seclusion in later years. All might have done differently and perhaps done better at another time, but what they did achieve has absolute as well as historical value and the vitality in the work of the best poets of the movement is far from being exhausted.

[1] Preface to *Poems*, 1853.
[2] Mrs Browning's *Sonnets from the Portuguese*, exceptionally personal poetry, were published under a title which suggested that they were translations. In these poems she spoke from the heart but her approach, techniques and accomplishment were not those of the Pre-Raphaelites with whose sonnets hers can most naturally be compared (as chapter 7 will demonstrate).

III

I shut myself in with my soul
And the shapes come eddying forth.

(Rossetti)

Self-expressive impulses are at the heart of the pheno-
menon known as Pre-Raphaelitism and they motivate the
poetry of Dante Gabriel Rossetti. What follows in this
book will be an attempt to identify and describe the forms
which self-expression took in Rossetti's work and the
patterns of thought and imagination which there were in
him to express. It is not necessary to claim that Rossetti is
a great poet to justify a study which concentrates on his
poetry. He had qualities of originality and imagination
touching greatness but his best gifts are confined to a
small area. This limitation which restricts his achievement is, from another point of view, the chief claim his
poetry has to be valued. The region where his imagination works most strongly and effectively is a sensitive
and secluded one. He writes of the reception of experience
in a part of the inner life where the protections of ordinary living are discarded and emotions such as pain and
ecstasy, guilt and fear are felt in their full power. Most
people never penetrate to such a point in themselves.
Rossetti's originality is to have visited it often and to
have sought words and images to describe it. The
achievement of his poetic imagination is that he often
succeeds. The ground he walks at his strongest belongs
to the same region that John Webster sighted when in
The Duchess of Malfi he made the Cardinal say:

> Whenever I look into the fish-ponds in my garden,
> Me thinks I see a thing armed with a rake,
> Which seems to strike at me.

It is a territory where images are the only language and
where strange and compelling sights are to be seen.

To define this area is not to encompass the whole of Rossetti, however. He had wit, intelligence, great technical resource and skill. These qualities sustain a poem like 'The Burden of Nineveh', for example, and give point and vitality to 'A Last Confession' and 'Jenny' but even in such poems, where more extravert gifts are called into play, there is invariably present, also, that distinctive imaginative touch which is a hallmark of Rossetti's writing.

Intelligence, perhaps, ought to be specially noticed in an introduction to Rossetti for he is often set down as an unthinking man. It is true that he was not an organised or systematic thinker but he had what may be described as a very intelligent imagination and he was responsive to the ideas and intellectual interests of his time to a far greater extent than has been recognised. He was capable of considerable penetration and arrived at some psychological and philosophical insights by sheer imaginative pressure before formal thinkers found their way to them. The evidence of this will be presented in chapter 2.

He was a divided man, sensitive to two worlds, the nineteenth-century one of Darwin and commerce and the medieval one of Dante with its clear anathema on the world, the flesh and the devil. His Italian ancestry may have deepened the gulf between science and materialism and mystery and spirit but if so this means only that he presents a sharper version of a situation experienced by many in a post-industrial, technological society. There are special psychological elements in Rossetti's position and he himself puts them before us both dramatically and subtly in his writing but he is also, to a not negligible extent, historically representative, like Tennyson and Arnold among others, of mid-nineteenth-century crisis. It is a mistake to treat him simply as a sport from the main root of Victorian life and literature. To do so weakens understanding of him and appreciation of his work and also impoverishes the Victorian scene. In this book I shall try to bring out what he shares with contemporaries although, of course, in the last analysis all comparisons must lead to recognition that it is his capacity to enlarge and illuminate as no one else can which makes a poet worth considering at all. To make Rossetti's case in those terms is the principal endeavour of the following study.

I

Dante draws an angel

THE most obvious aspects of Rossetti's life and career invite description in terms of a duality. He was born and bred in England but by parentage he was three-quarters Italian. He made his living as a painter but he was also a poet. Like most gifts, Rossetti's endowments were mixed blessings. To live in nineteenth-century England surrounded in youth by Italian exiles, to translate not only Dante but also, *con amore*, the lyrics of his contemporaries and predecessors, guarantees some width of view and at least a measure of immunity from damaging forms of Victorianism, but it is likely also to produce disorientation and a spiritual alienation from both communities. A man who both paints and writes poetry is specially favoured of the gods but divided allegiance and divided attention may starve both gifts. Later critics have sometimes applied to Rossetti's career as poet-painter the title of one of his sonnets from *The House of Life*, 'Lost on Both Sides'.

The theme of duality can be taken much further than these observations suggest and it leads to more interesting discoveries than the mere recognition of separate sets of competing claims. It leads, in fact, to a view of the world of Rossetti's imagination which shows it to be rather different in kind and wider in dimension than is commonly supposed. The focus of attention in this book will be on the poetry with only subsidiary reference to the painting but to study Rossetti's imagination through only one of his arts involves no fundamental distortion, for the impulses at work in both are the same. Poetry, in the nature of the case, is more articulate and, because it was not Rossetti's means of earning his living, it was also a more consistently intimate expression of his innermost self. The relationship between the arts in Rossetti's career can be illustrated with the help of an episode from Dante's *Vita Nuova*, a very appropriate source of illumination, for Dante's influence on Rossetti is pervasive in his work, early and late.

Rossetti first published his translation of the *Vita Nuova* in 1861, in a volume entitled *The Early Italian Poets*, but he began work on it when he was very young[1] and at various times he illustrated scenes from it. One such attempt dates from the year when he was twenty-one. It is a drawing, now in Birmingham Art Gallery, of the episode in which the young Dante, alone in his room on the first anniversary of his lady's death and inspired by her memory, began to draw the figure of an angel. He was so absorbed in transferring his vision to the panel that he failed for some time to notice that visitors had come into the room and were watching him at work. When they had left him, he turned back to his drawing but then decided instead to write a poem, addressed to the visitors. In the poem he would explain to them that it was because of his strong sense of the presence of the dead Beatrice that he was for so long unaware of their arrival. Rossetti painted the scene as a water-colour in 1853[2] and there is an even earlier drawing than the one in Birmingham;[3] but the Birmingham version is particularly interesting. It is signed 'Dante G. Rossetti P.R.B. 1849'

[1] Rossetti had completed his translation by November 1848 – see *Letters*, i, p. 48. *The Early Italian Poets* was reissued in 1874 in a rearranged form and with a new title, *Dante and His Circle*.

[2] Surtees no. 58; reproduced in O. Doughty, *A Victorian Romantic* (2nd edition, Oxford, 1960), facing p. 192.

[3] A. I. Grieve, in the first part of his work on Rossetti as artist, *The Pre-Raphaelite Period 1848–50* (Real World Publications, Norwich, 1973), reproduces the earlier drawing, dated September 1848. Grieve comments that Rossetti 'has managed to suggest in his figures, particularly in Dante and his principal visitor, a new feeling of intense mental drama'; but the 1849 drawing is more developed and much more effective.

and inscribed 'Dante G. Rossetti to his P.R. Brother
John E. Millais'. In all its versions the essence of the
scene is the invasion of a private by a public world and
the angular lines of the 1849 drawing convey the drama
particularly effectively. The young Dante, in the act of
rising and turning round, meets half-abashed the steady
gaze of the man in the foreground. Two other men
whisper surreptitious comments. A small page with no
interest in the proceedings scratches his right leg with
the pointed toe of his left shoe. The sense of intrusion is
made acute by the head which pokes forward inquisitively
to peer at the panel on which Dante is painting and in so
doing violates the space, about a third of the whole,
which belongs to Dante. The whole drawing is a very
striking representation of the disruption, even the
desecration, of a private vision and moment of communion by an unsympathetic, uncomprehending, invad-
ing, outer world. Rossetti's translation of the text reflects
the same sense of painful collision between inner and
outer worlds. He throws emphasis on to the intensity of
Dante's visionary communion with Beatrice and renders
the words in which Dante excuses himself to his visitors
for his absent-mindedness by the simple 'Another was
with me'. In a note he explains that he has rejected the
continuation which most texts add, 'And therefore was I
in thought', because 'the shorter speech is perhaps the
more forcible and pathetic'.[1] He did not wish to dilute
Dante's simple affirmation of the communion of his soul
with Beatrice, and the effect of the concision is to heighten
the contrast between the inwardness represented by the
painting and the outward turning to the visitors which
results in a poem of explanation.

The same episode interested Browning who supplies
his own gloss on Dante's unfamiliar role as painter in his
poem 'One Word More'. To express the most intimate
of his feelings, Browning suggests, an artist may turn

[1] *Works*, ii, p. 84.

away from the medium in which with practised skill he
displays his art to the world and Dante's picture if he had
finished it would have had a more direct relation to
Dante the man than *The Divine Comedy* could have. The
artist practising the art in which he has name and fame
can never escape from the expectations that surround
him and he may find greater release for his personal
feelings in some unfamiliar mode:

> Does he paint? he fain would write a poem –
> Does he write? he fain would paint a picture.

The poem is a celebration of romantic love and is addressed
to Mrs Browning:

> You and I would rather see that angel,
> Painted by the tenderness of Dante,
> Would we not? – than read a fresh Inferno.

> You and I will never see that picture.
> While he mused on love and Beatrice,
> While he softened o'er his outline angel,
> In they broke, those 'people of importance':
> We and Bice bear the loss for ever.

Browning's poem treats the episode as an example of
distinction between public and private art and the poem,
together with Rossetti's drawing, is very suggestive about
the relation of poetry to painting in Rossetti's career.
Though the situation may not be as clear-cut as perhaps
it was for Dante, there is an effective difference between
the status of the two arts in Rossetti's career all the same.
In middle age Rossetti decided to come before the public
as poet as well as painter but he had been writing for
many years before that and published little. The appearance of the 1870 volume was equivalent to opening the
door of his sanctum to the visitors from outside. He did
it of his own free will, not surprised like Dante at his
drawing, but the decision caused him a great deal of
anxiety nevertheless. He was painfully careful in the
preparation of the volume and in the end his reactions to

hostile criticism were so severe as to undermine his health and precipitate his death. The critics who, like official visitors, have walked into the private room since, have behaved much like the intruders in the Dante sketch although Rossetti at work delineating his private vision deserves more respect.

The young Rossetti urged his friends to paint. In poetry, he thought, everything had been done, especially by Keats. 'If any man has any poetry in him he should paint it', he told his young disciples. 'The next Keats ought to be a painter.'[1] Keats with his fidelity to the 'Principle of Beauty' and his distrust of 'the consecutive reason', his faith that the imaginative perception of Beauty is also 'Truth', seemed to embody the essential spirit of Romanticism which had opened up a new world for poetry. The play of Keats's intense imagination upon sense objects, the rich colouring and strong feeling of his poems made a strong appeal to the young Pre-Raphaelites and 'The Eve of St. Agnes', was a particular favourite. In painting they could see no such quickening and releasing impulse. Artists were still constrained by outworn laws – hence it was the revivifying of painting which the little group of art students, Rossetti and a few friends, undertook in 1848. Nevertheless when the youthful Pre-Raphaelite Brotherhood sought to sow the seed of reform by its magazine, *The Germ*, Rossetti insisted that their programme should include literature as well as art and he wrote poetry for *The Germ* and stimulated his friends to do so. When he wrote about painting in these years, his mind turned easily to poetry for comparison and illustration. Commenting on 'The Rival's Wedding' by Anthony, he writes: 'After contemplating the picture for some while, it will gradually produce that indefinable sense of rest and wonder which, when childhood is once gone, poetry alone can recall. And assuredly, before he knew that colour was laid on with brushes, or that oil

[1] Doughty, *A Victorian Romantic*, p. 209.

painting was done upon canvas, this painter was a poet.'[1] 'This picture', he wrote of another, 'should hang in the room of a poet: we will dare to say that Keats himself might have lain dreaming before it, and found it minister to his inspiration.'[2] The primacy of the poetic imagination is implied in both these comments but for many years painting absorbed his professional attention.

His painting was always intended for the market but his poetry, for the greater part, he kept to himself till he was forty-two. He might, in fact, have published rather earlier for the volume of *Early Italian Poets* in 1861 carried an announcement of a collection to be called *Dante at Verona and Other Poems*. Rossetti had been hesitating over this step for some time but in the event his plan to bring his poetry before the public gave way to a startling demonstration of how intimately his work in this other art was linked with his private life. His wife died suddenly in 1862 and in grief and dismay he had his manuscripts buried in the coffin with her. Seven years later, in the flush of a revival of poetic inspiration, the coffin was opened and the manuscripts removed so that he could build up, out of the work of more than twenty years, the volume which appeared in 1870.

Why did he change his mind and offer to the world his private art? There is nothing mysterious about this. Together with the artist's compulsion to express himself fully, there goes the urge to leave as legacies to the world the conceptions, the images of reality as he has experienced it, which are uniquely his to give. Certainly Rossetti felt this impulse. In August 1871 he wrote revealingly to Bell Scott about a desire 'really [to] get one's brain into print before one died'.[3] He was thinking about the possibility of having one of his paintings lithographed but the choice of words suggests an attitude which has wider relevance.

[1] *Works*, ii, p. 492.
[2] Ibid., p. 495
[3] *Letters*, iii, p. 992.

The same kind of emphasis occurs again three years later when he comments to Ford Madox Brown on the painter Regnault and draws attention to his want of 'brain': 'I think that his mind dwelt chiefly on externals available for painting of a startling kind, though he had intellect enough to persuade himself that he thought.'[1] Rossetti himself has often been accused of dealing chiefly with externals of a startling kind, but his ambition at least was greater than this. Perhaps he felt that his lack of full technical proficiency impeded his getting his brain into his painting and so he committed himself to getting his poetry into print in the most perfect possible form, before he died.[2] Perhaps he agreed with Shelley: 'language… is a more direct representation of the actions and passions of our internal being, and is susceptible of more various and delicate combinations than colour, form, or motion, and is more plastic and obedient to the control of that faculty of which it is the creation'.[3] He had always felt the need to supplement the images of his paintings by words, as the sonnets written for paintings show, and by 1870 he felt an urgent need for the fuller expressiveness which he believed he could attain in poetry. 'My own

---

[1] Ibid., p. 1278.

[2] On this point W. M. Rossetti quotes a letter of his brother's, from 1877, and comments:

> Rossetti, being a painter with high ideals in art, and an earnest desire to work in conformity to those ideals, was not contented with what he actually produced. He knew it to be good and skilful up to a certain point; but there was a loftier point to which his ideal and his conception reached, and which his hand had not reached.

Dante Gabriel Rossetti: His Family-Letters with a Memoir (London, 1895), i, p. 352.

[3] 'A Defence of Poetry' (*Prose Works of Shelley* edited by R. H. Shepherd London, 1966), ii, p. 6). Wilde repeated the point in characteristic style:

> Words have not merely music as sweet as that of viol and lute, colour as rich and vivid as any that makes lovely for us the canvas of the Venetian or the Spaniard, and plastic form no less sure and certain than that which reveals itself in marble or in bronze, but thought and passion and spirituality are theirs also, are theirs indeed alone.

'The Critic as Artist', in *Intentions*, 1891.

B

belief is that I am a poet...primarily', he wrote to Thomas Hake in 1870, 'and that it is my poetic tendencies that chiefly give value to my pictures: only', he added, 'painting being – what poetry is not – a livelihood, I have put my poetry chiefly in that form.'[1] A year later he wrote in similar vein to Ford Madox Brown: 'I wish one could live by writing poetry. I think I'd see painting damned if one could.'[2]

So the private art was brought out in public for the world to see and Robert Buchanan thrust his face in, like the man in the drawing, and peered with sceptical eyes at what the poet had been doing. Having looked, he denounced Rossetti. It was no angel he had been delineating, he reported, but a satyr. The history of Buchanan's attack on Rossetti in *The Fleshly School of Poetry*[3] and of Rossetti's reply, *The Stealthy School of Criticism*,[4] is well-known but not the less important and interesting for that. Rossetti's poetry, Buchanan asserted, aimed to 'extol fleshliness as the distinct and supreme end of poetic and pictorial art; aver that poetic expression is greater than poetic thought; and by inference, that the body is greater than the soul, and sound superior to sense'. To Rossetti, who was interested in getting his brain into print and who castigated Regnault for his lack of thought, the accusations were preposterous as well as being the most damaging possible to his conception of himself and his work. His reply is dignified and able but the exchange raises questions which neither Buchanan nor Rossetti himself satisfactorily settled. For when Rossetti opened the door on his inner life by publishing his poetry, his private art, he exposed not only moments of intense

---

[1] *Letters* ii, p. 849.

[2] *Letters* iii, p. 996.

[3] Buchanan's attack first appeared as an article in the *Contemporary Review* for October 1871 and was reissued in expanded form as a pamphlet in 1872.

[4] Rossetti's reply was first published in the *Athenaeum* and is reprinted in *Works*, i, pp. 480–8.

visionary insight, his equivalent of the young Dante's vision of Beatrice, but also the counter-images which always threatened to overwhelm his vision. Rossetti's angels *could* be satyrs and Buchanan was right to catch the grimace. He was wrong to think it a permanent feature. Rossetti was right to rebut the charge but the poetry itself tells a fuller story than his reply to Buchanan does. This book will attempt to decipher that story and to characterise more accurately than has been done before the nature of the image which Rossetti's private art of poetry delineates.

If we turn to specific examples of work where Rossetti's imagination as both painter and poet is engaged we can see more clearly how the poetry takes us across thresholds where the painting stops short. One of the most interesting examples of this kind is the poem called 'The Portrait', the first version of which dates from the time when Rossetti was nineteen. The 'I' of the poem is an artist and he is looking at a picture that he once painted of his beloved who is now dead. 'This is her picture as she was', the poem begins and the plain statement and the forceful use of the verb 'to be' link it in style with such other early poems as 'Mary's Girlhood', a sonnet written for Rossetti's painting 'Ecce Ancilla Domini', and 'My Sister's Sleep'. The strength of 'Mary's Girlhood' lies in the quiet factual treatment of the great mystery of the moment when Mary learnt that she should become the Mother of God. 'My Sister's Sleep' uses a similar technique; its dramatic impact derives from the keen physical recreation of a common-place scene as the setting for the mysteries of human death and divine birth. In both poems the mystery is implicit, unstressed, and the emphasis lies on what can be expressed through physical detail or simple statement. A sense is nevertheless strongly evoked of the vast perspectives in which the sharply focused scenes are set.

Though 'The Portrait' begins in the style of these

poems, by the time we reach the third stanza it is clear
that Rossetti is aiming in this poem for different effects.
'In painting her', the poet-painter of the poem tells us:

> . . . I shrined her face
> 'Mid mystic trees, where light falls in
> Hardly at all; a covert place
> Where you might think to find a din
> Of doubtful talk, and a live flame
> Wandering, and many a shape whose name
> Not itself knoweth, and old dew,
> And your own footsteps meeting you,
> And all things going as they came.

Mystery is directly conveyed by the choice of language
and reference in these lines. When he painted his beloved
the artist placed her, not in a real-life setting which could
be treated with homely detail, but in some shadowy
interior landscape where shape and sound and common
things have put off their familiar nature and lost their
definition. The stanza recalls Rossetti's painting 'How
they met Themselves',[1] in which lovers walking in a dark
wood meet their doubles and the woman falls back
appalled, recognising, it seems, her imminent death in
the image of herself she sees before her. But after the
mystic wood of stanza three, we discover in stanza four
that in fact there was a real wood and that the lover and
his lady walked there on one specific day – 'in *that* wood
that day'. The poet then goes on to add circumstantial
detail which enhances the realism of the situation as it is
now presented. He recalls how, on that day, when he was
about to declare his love, a storm broke and prevented
him; but in the evening, indoors, he spoke:

> That eve I spoke those words again
> Beside the pelted window-pane;
> And there she hearkened what I said,
> With under-glances that surveyed
> The empty pastures blind with rain.

[1] Surtees, no. 118.

Mystery at this point has vanished and we seem to be back with the kind of accurate and evocative description which distinguishes 'My Sister's Sleep' and the annunciation poem.

Up to this point in the poem, the wood has been in turn a mystic landscape existing apart from time and place and a real wood in which real people walked on an actual day. In stanza seven, the wood image becomes something else again:

> Next day the memories of these things,
> Like leaves through which a bird has flown,
> Still vibrated with Love's warm wings . . .

The image of a bird flying through thickly leaved trees in a grove or wood is one which recurs in Rossetti's poetry to denote a deep private experience. It is beautiful here, as always, and it is effective, but these successive appearances of the wood – a mystic place where doppelgänger may walk, a real wood, and an image for delicate and intimate feeling – unsettle the outlines of a poem which began so positively and leave uncertain the boundary between physical reality and subjective experience.

The second half of stanza seven, after the simile related to love, proceeds on a matter-of-fact level. To perpetuate the memory of the day in the wood and the moments when love was avowed, the lover decides to paint a picture. And so:

> She stood among the plants in bloom
> At windows of a summer room,
> To feign the shadow of the trees.

It comes as something of a surprise to find that the shade thrown by the 'mystic trees' of stanza three was in reality thrown by house-plants standing in windows filled with sunshine and that the whole atmosphere in which the portrait was painted was throbbing with life and love:

> It seemed each sun-thrilled blossom there
> Beat like a heart among the leaves.

Yet the girl, we already know, is dead, and the end of the same stanza reminds us of this:

> O heart that never beats nor heaves,
> In that one darkness lying still,
> What now to thee my love's great will
> Or the fine web the sunshine weaves?

The trees may have been house-plants and the sun may have been shining when the picture was painted but the double whom the girl saw in the strange wood when, the picture completed, she could see herself imaged in it, was in fact a harbinger of death. At this point the wood appears once more in the poem, a mystic place indeed, found in the heart of an inner landscape which the lover wanders through at night, as he lies in his bed striving to regain contact with the past:

> Last night at last I could have slept,
> And yet delayed my sleep till dawn,
> Still wandering. Then it was I wept:
> For unawares I came upon
> Those glades where once she walked with me:
> And as I stood there suddenly,
> All wan with traversing the night,
> Upon the desolate verge of light
> Yearned loud the iron-bosomed sea.

It is possible that these lines refer to physical experience and that the lover is not in bed but literally wandering through the night. Such ambiguity is typical of the poem where planes of reality merge into each other but the metaphorical meaning seems the dominant one. On this reading the stanza marks the furthest reach of the poem. The action has moved right away from physical life and locality to an interior deep in the mind, a point on the very verge of eternity.

> Consider the sea's listless chime:
> Time's self it is, made audible

Rossetti writes in the lyric, 'The Sea Limits', and the

symbolic function of the sea in 'The Portrait' is evident. The lover *almost* attains reunion with his beloved across the frontier of death but an inexorable awareness of time frustrates the full communion. This last experience of the wood, however, seems to him to prefigure his ultimate arrival and reuniting with the beloved in heaven.

The poem epitomises a characteristic process of Rossetti's imagination. It has a physical experience at its root, a lovers' walk through a wood, an exchange of vows, a death. This experience is translated into a painting, a portrait of a girl so lifelike that it almost seems to live. Yet the picture is more than a simple record of physical reality for the artist's imagination has transformed the real setting of sunshine and light into one of mystery and doom. The picture, therefore, creates a world of its own, investing the portrait of the girl with suggestion and implication not at all connected with representational art. The commentary of the painter-lover-become-poet brings out for our recognition the two kinds of perception which the painting embodies. His ambivalent treatment of the wood reproduces in the poem the shift of planes of reality which is effected in the painting. So far, poem and painting keep pace with each other but then the poem goes further. The poet takes the whole experience deep into his mind and there, in some psychic region, he finds again *that* wood *that* day, and approaches a vision of the timelessness of crucial experiences existing eternally in spite of time. What Rossetti once called 'the value of monumental moments'[1] is on one level a part of the preoccupation with time which he shared with his contemporaries; on another it is part of his own visionary mysticism. In 'The Portrait' the night-time return to the wood leads to two final stanzas in which the unorthodox intimation of immortality given in stanza ten is transformed into what is, ostensibly at least, the more orthodox terminology of a Christian heaven.

[1] *Works*, i, p. 511.

The poem written by the artist-poet persona explores further into his experience of love and death than the picture, on which the poem is a commentary, would evidently do. Similarly the poem leads us deeper into the territory of Rossetti's imagination than the painting 'How They Met Themselves' does. It is a territory whose landmarks are images – birds, woods, spring-water and streams – recurrent throughout his poetry as the vocabulary of his deepest experience. The images are not arcane and within 'The Portrait' the poem itself fully establishes their values. Yet they can be overlooked or misunderstood and they have been. Some unsympathetic comments on the penultimate stanza provide a case in point and are worth attention because the issue they raise has implications for much of Rossetti's poetry.

After the momentary but imperfect revelation of stanza ten, the poem continues:

> Even so, where Heaven holds breath and hears
> The beating heart of Love's own breast, –
> Where round the secret of all spheres
> All angels lay their wings to rest, –
> How shall my soul stand rapt and awed,
> When, by the new birth borne abroad
> Throughout the music of the suns,
> It enters in her soul at once
> And knows the silence there for God!

This is the weakest stanza in the poem. Its images and language quite lack the quality of precision hand in hand with mystery which characterises the rest of the poem, but Mr R. D. Waller in his book, *The Rossetti Family*,[1] has judged otherwise. He has high praise for the stanza but finds serious fault with the last two lines: 'Had Rossetti been questioned about the last two lines of this otherwise very beautiful stanza, could he have explained them in terms either of literal belief, or of metaphorical imagination?' he asks, and in a footnote he suggests that if they

[1] Manchester, 1932.

have meaning it is 'nothing more than the sexual embrace writ fairer in terms of heaven and made altogether ineffable'.[1] Mr Waller has been felt, by other critics of the poem, to make a shrewd point when he questions the meaning of Rossetti's lines but his whole commentary on this stanza seems to indicate, on the contrary, a total misunderstanding. The last two lines are much more consonant with the poem as a whole than the lines which Mr Waller praises and to ask for an explanation of them *either* in terms of literal belief *or* of metaphorical imagination is to imply ignorance of the nature of a poem which is continually crossing from the literal to the non-literal. When the soul of the lover after death encounters once again the beloved and

> enters in her soul at once
> And knows the silence there for God

the words need to be taken in the context of a poem which has put forward all along the idea of landscapes of the soul. When the lover and his beloved tread these mystic regions of the soul together, they will no longer be troubled by the yearnings of the iron-bosomed sea of time which held them apart while he lived on after her death, for time will be lost in God's eternity and the yearnings of the time-bound human being will at last be silenced. The lines are not nonsense though they do indeed belong to the strange and distinctive world of Rossetti's imagination. Its strangeness and distinctiveness are such that the plainest of its landmarks have often gone unrecognised, as they were by Mr Waller.

The occult suggestions in 'The Portrait' are far from being exceptional in Rossetti's work. In this poem, the seeing of one's image is a signal of imminent death and death and portraiture are again closely connected in the story, *Saint Agnes of Intercession*, which Rossetti wrote for *The Germ*. How the main story would have developed is

[1] Ibid., pp. 204–5.

uncertain since it was never finished but the story of the imaginary fifteenth-century painter Bucciuolo Angiolieri, on which it would almost certainly have been modelled, strongly connects the painter's image-making with death. Angiolieri, whose beloved lies dying, comes to her in Lucca: 'When on his arrival, she witnessed his anguish at thus losing her for ever, Blanzifiore declared that she would rise at once from her bed, and that Bucciuolo should paint her portrait before she died; for so, she said, there should still remain something to him whereby to have her in memory.' For two days, 'though in a dying state, she sat with wonderful energy to her lover . . . On the third day, while Bucciuolo was still at work, she died without moving.'[1] This is the portrait in which the modern hero of the story recognises the exact likeness of the girl he himself loves. There is a similar episode in Poe's story, *The Oval Portrait*, in which a husband paints his young bride, but the episode is there more sinister for he is literally, though unintentionally, drawing her life from her as he works: 'for one moment, the painter stood entranced before the work which he had wrought; but in the next, while he yet gazed, he grew tremulous and very pallid, and aghast, and crying with a loud voice, "This is indeed *Life* itself!" turned suddenly to regard his beloved:– *She was dead*!' Rossetti may have known the story and his mind turned naturally all his life towards the mystic, the mysterious, the occult. For the ballad *Sister Helen*, first published in 1881, he used the old folk-lore superstition of the melting of a wax image of the victim as a way of destroying a life. The latest and earliest published work is thus linked by a

---

[1] *Works*, i, p. 415. William Michael Rossetti in his 1911 edition of the *Works of D. G. Rossetti* records that his brother began an etching to illustrate *Saint Agnes of Intercession* but threw it aside. Millais, however, did one which 'manifestly represents the hero of the story painting the portrait of his affianced bride during her mortal illness. This, therefore, is clearly shown to be the intended *finale* of the tale; as indeed one might readily divine from that portion of it which was written'.

common interest in the mystic connection between the visual representation and the person represented but, more commonly, the mystery that he found in portraiture was of a different kind.

The locations in 'The Portrait' are partly physical, partly psychic, and the octave of sonnet no. x of *The House of Life* (written in 1868)[1] makes use of the same imagery of a landscape of the soul:

> O Lord of all compassionate control,
> O Love! let this my lady's picture glow
> Under my hand to praise her name, and show
> Even of her inner self the perfect whole:
> That he who seeks her beauty's furthest goal,
> Beyond the light that the sweet glances throw
> And refluent wave of the sweet smile, may know
> The very sky and sea-line of her soul.

This sonnet, like the earlier poem, is also called 'The Portrait' though it probably relates, unlike the other, to a real picture. The subject of the sonnet is likely to be one of those portraits of Jane Morris which Rossetti painted plentifully in later years. 'The shadowed eyes remember and foresee', the sestet tells us, a line which might apply to many of them. 'Proserpine' is an oil painting of Jane Morris, dated 1874,[2] and for this Rossetti wrote two accompanying sonnets, one in English, one in Italian. It is a striking painting and the poems take us into the mind of the woman, telling us what she is thinking as she stands brooding, with the bitten fruit in her hand. Seized one day from the upper world, as she was gathering flowers in the spring in Sicily, and forced now to dwell in the kingdom of the underworld with its dark ruler, Dis, she laments her state:

---

[1] Dates given for sonnets from *The House of Life* will be dates of composition as listed by W. E. Fredeman in 'Rossetti's *In Memoriam*: an Elegiac Reading of *The House of Life*', *Bulletin of the John Rylands Library*, 47, 1964–5, pp. 298–341.

[2] Surtees, no. 233.

> Afar away the light that brings cold cheer
> Unto this wall – one instant and no more
> Admitted at my distant palace-door.
> Afar the flowers of Enna from this drear
> Dire fruit, which, tasted once, must thrall me here.
> Afar those skies from this Tartarean grey
> That chills me: and afar, how far away,
> The nights that shall be from the days that were.

So far the poem is plain sailing. The octave both recalls the story and creates an atmosphere for the painting; but the sestet goes further:

> Afar from mine own self I seem, and wing
> Strange ways in thought, and listen for a sign:
> And still some heart unto some soul doth pine,
> (Whose sounds mine inner sense is fain to bring,
> Continually together murmuring,)
> 'Woe's me for thee, unhappy Proserpine!'[1]

The bird image indicates at once the kind of experience which Rossetti means to evoke. The woman is not merely unhappy at her lot but the poem directs us to see that her eyes are looking into that interior world whose mysterious depths the lover of the earlier 'Portrait' poem came upon and to which so many paths in the world of Rossetti's imagination lead.

Rossetti made sketches and more finished drawings of members of his family, and of friends and acquaintances, but the paintings of women based on his favourite female models, mystic portraits as they may be called, have

---

[1] The Italian and English versions of the sonnet are close, except at lines 9–10. The Italian has no comparable image to the English and reads:

> Lungi da me mi sento; e ognor sognando
> Cerco e ricerco, e resto ascoltatrice.

Rossetti's sister Maria wrote to him about the poems:

> Graceful and melodious as is your English sonnet, I agree with you in preferring the Italian. But no wonder; for, as it is thought and character that create language, thoughts that would more naturally take birth in an Italian than in an English character will of course find the most fitting expression in Italian.

Quoted by Helen Rossetti Angeli, *Dante Gabriel Rossetti* (London, 1949), p. 257.

other intentions than to capture a scene or a personality.[1]
In a poem, however, something like psychological
analysis may take place, as it does in the Proserpina
sonnets. 'Lungi da me mi sento', 'Afar from mine own
self I seem': Proserpina, wrenched suddenly from one
world to another, describes her situation at first in terms
of the physical images of the octave, but in the sestet the
images relate to inner experience and describe her sense
of loss of identity. The birds from the inner covert of the
soul are disoriented and recognise no landmarks. She is
aware of heart and soul as disjoined elements of her
shattered personality and can only dimly think of herself
as some third person, 'unhappy Proserpine'. The eyes of
the figure in the painting gaze past us at some view we
could never hope to see but the images of the poem
reveal to us how Rossetti interpreted her experience and
enable us to participate in it.

The sonnets for 'Proserpine', the early 'Portrait' poem
and the sonnet from *The House of Life* illustrate the two
main aspects of the 'mystery' which stimulated Rossetti's
imagination when he painted these portraits, either in
words or on canvas. At one time he is concerned with
the psychological drama, the inner world behind the
eyes, as he is in 'Proserpina'. At another, the stress falls
on the relation of the individual to ambient powers –
Beauty and Love, as in the sonnet from *The House of Life*,
or, it may be, less benign forces. The poetry enables us
to identify and explore these regions of experience and to
recognise also that, though the emphasis may fall differ-

[1] L. S. Lowry was, perhaps rather surprisingly, a keen admirer of Rossetti.
'There is no one like Rossetti', he said –

> I don't care much for his subject pictures but his women are very
> wonderful. I can't find anything quite like them. The Old Masters
> didn't quite get them . . . They're very queer creatures and I like him
> for it . . . What he puts into the individual is all him, not the individual,
> they're probably very ordinary people.

(Quoted in *A Pre-Raphaelite Passion: The Private Collection of L. S. Lowry*,
Manchester City Art Gallery catalogue of an exhibition held 1 April–
31 May 1977.)

ently at various times, the 'mystery' is really indivisible. Penetration of the individual psyche invariably leads to questions of the relation of the individual to death and life, time and eternity, good and evil. Psychological analysis in Rossetti's poems is not clinical but attached to memory and desire, or, to grief, guilt and remorse. Proserpina herself is a victim of darkness and remembers the light. She has bound herself to the underworld by eating the fruit she found there and her personality is torn between a lost world of purity and a present domain of corruption. The flowers of Enna and the kingdom of Dis symbolise the forces which pull and tear the individual soul aspiring to light but enthralled to darkness. To translate the poem in this way is to indicate the frame of reference in which it needs to be seen for, to Rossetti, the image of Proserpina throbs with the mystery of life, mirroring both the strange ways of thought which the individual mind follows and the unknown powers which surround it. The poem interprets the painting and adds a dimension to it as, in a similar fashion, the painter-poet of 'The Portrait' interpreted and added to the meaning of his painting till he brought his poem to an ecstatic culmination in the penultimate stanza.

Rossetti's performance as a painter, whatever his natural strengths and limitations may have been, was subject to control by the demands of the market and the taste of patrons. Poetry was the art, as he put it, 'in which I have done no pot-boiling at any rate'.[1] In the relative freedom of his poetry he used image and symbol to map the world of his inner experience. It is a map worth studying and one, like medieval examples, embellished with angels and monsters. In Rossetti's world, however, it is sometimes difficult to tell which is which.

2
A man of his time

'IT has often seemed to me that all work, to be truly worthy, should be wrought out of the age itself, as well as out of the soul of its producer, which must needs be a soul of the age.'[1] These words, by the young narrator of *Saint Agnes of Intercession*, might seem to cut him off quite sharply from his creator whose painting and poetry are full of medieval subjects and whose imagination scarcely seems at home in nineteenth-century industrial England. It is notorious, for example, that Rossetti's one attempt at a contemporary subject in painting, 'Found', was never completed. In some essential ways Rossetti was a stranger in his time and place but nevertheless in other respects he stands firmly in the midst of Victorian life and literature. To ignore his place in context does him no service, for it tends to make him seem merely odd and obscures his real originality.

He shared with others, for example, a serious concern about the place and function of art. Three sonnets, written in 1848–9 and later included in *The House of Life* with the title 'Old and New Art', give us the reflections of a serious and even rather priggish young man. The first, sub-titled 'St Luke the Painter', is the most interesting since it offers a sonnet-size history of art. When artists first, it tells us, sought to put their gifts at the service of religion, they confined themselves to specifically religious images. Then they learned that the whole created world could be seen as a symbol of the divine:

> . . . sky-breadth and field-silence and this day
> Are symbols also in some deeper way

[1] *Works*, i, p. 402.

37

and with this realisation their art reached its peak. Later still, their inspiration waned and they merely imitated what had been done before – 'soulless self-reflections of man's skill' – but there may yet be time, in the evening of the world, to find once more the authentic vision. The poem adopts the language of piety but its relevance to Rossetti's view of his own mission as artist, in the heyday of the Pre-Raphaelite Brotherhood, is clear enough. The uninspired imitators who have lost the energy and sincerity of their predecessors are the post-Raphaelite painters, especially those nurtured in the Royal Academy schools, and the young Pre-Raphaelites must go back to beginnings and 'pray again' to revive the inspiration which animated the masters of the past.

The other two sonnets, 'Not as These' and 'The Husbandmen', respectively admonish and encourage the aspiring young man. He should be humble in contemplation of the painters of 'the great Past' in whose steps he longs to follow but he should not despair though he comes late into the field, like those workers in the parable who missed the heat of the day in the vineyard. They also earned their penny and to the young men of 1848 there may be destined a greater reward, to reclaim British art from atrophy by the inspiration of the early painters:

> Which of ye knoweth *he* is not that last
> Who may be first by faith and will? – yea, his
> The hand which after the appointed days
> And hours shall give a Future to their Past?

These are a young man's poems and they voice unmistakably the mood and circumstances of the time when they were written. Yet more than thirty years later Rossetti still thought them worthy of inclusion in the latest, 1881 version of *The House of Life*. Whatever the religious terminology meant to him by that time, he believed more than ever in symbols communicating 'in some deeper way' deep truths. Though he might wish in some moods to 'see painting damned' it was only for the sake of cultivating his other gift of poetry. He never failed to take art itself seriously.

The story 'Hand and Soul' was written at about the same time as the sonnets and it expands the thinking behind them. It is the story of a young man of Arezzo, some time in the Middle Ages, who from his boyhood deeply loves art. 'The extreme longing after a visible embodiment of his thought strengthened as his years increased'[1] and at the age of nineteen the youth goes to Pisa to meet one Giunta Pisano who has a great reputation as an artist. But when he looks at his work he feels, like the young man in the second of the sonnets, that he himself has the capacity to be the superior artist. He goes on to become a famous painter, spurred on to work by fear of others outstripping him, but, having reached the goal he had set himself, he is still dissatisfied. He had believed that his work was a form of worship and service, 'the peace-offering that he made to God and to his own soul for the eager selfishness of his aim',[2] but now he suspects that he had deceived himself: 'he became aware that much of that reverence which he had mistaken for faith had been no more than the worship of beauty'.[3] So he sets himself instead to painting pictures which will have no other end than 'the presentment of some moral greatness that should influence the beholder'.[4] This they signally fail to do. As he reaches a crisis of despair, a woman appears in his room. She is, as she tells him, the image of his own soul and her message is that he should labour on and trust to the gifts which God has given him: 'What He hath set in thine heart to do, that do thou; and even though thou do it without thought of Him, it shall be well done; it is this sacrifice that He asketh of thee, and His flame is upon it for a sign.'[5] Her

[1] *Works*, i, 384.
[2] Ibid., p. 387.
[3] Ibid.
[4] Ibid., p. 388.
[5] Ibid., p. 393.

manner of speech is somewhat oracular: 'Know that there is but this means whereby thou mayst serve God with man: Set thine hand and thy soul to serve man with God.'[1] She seems to be teaching the lesson which Art learned in 'St Luke the Painter', that the phenomena of nature are themselves symbols of God so that, as the sonnet puts it, 'She [Art] looked through these to God and was God's priest.'

The teachings about art and the artist are not the clearest and most striking things about 'Hand and Soul'. What lingers in the memory is the brilliant account of a feud between the two greatest houses in Pisa which is full of precisely imagined and dramatic detail, and also the description of the woman who is the image of Chiaro's soul. This vision of the woman constitutes the heart of the story. As a coda to the tale, Rossetti writes a little sophisticated modern scene in a picture gallery in which the mystical quality of the vision is treated with irony and scepticism but this is only to protect the vision itself from the mockery of unsympathetic readers. Rossetti cares very much, it is obvious, about the relation between hand and soul and, if the mystical figure is rather disappointingly wordy and not particularly lucid, at least the earnestness with which the young author was facing questions about his role as artist is perfectly plain.

Rossetti's youthful anxieties about art and the soul may have owed something to Tennyson whose allegorical poem, 'The Palace of Art', was first published in 1833. As the prefatory poem describes it, it tells

> . . . of a soul
> A sinful soul possess'd of many gifts,
> A spacious garden full of flowering weeds,
> A glorious Devil, large in heart and brain,
> That did love Beauty only . . .

The sinful soul revels at first in her palace of art but in

[1] Ibid., p. 394.

the end her arrogant isolation from the life of the world
and selfish indifference to 'the riddle of the painful earth'
bring retribution and her palace becomes a place of nightmare. She has to 'purge' her 'guilt' by humility and repen-
tance. Rossetti could never have written at any time of
his life that 'Beauty, Good, and Knowledge are three
sisters', as Tennyson claims, but the painter of 'Hand and
Soul' seems to have been infected with some of Tennyson's
tremors concerning the morality of beauty when he
'became aware that much of that reverence which he had
mistaken for faith had been no more than the worship of
beauty'. How legitimate the worship of beauty might be
and what consequences it could have in the life of the
worshipper were questions that pressed on Rossetti with
increasing urgency as he grew older but the dismissive
phraseology, *no more than* the worship of beauty' is never
repeated. It was always a more Tennysonian than
Rossettian formulation.

Rossetti continued to read Tennyson carefully and to
recognise his greatness but he was not impressed by
Tennyson in his more public-spirited mood. He thought
that there was 'glorious' poetry in 'Maud', especially the
garden scene (i, xxii), but he had strong reservations
about other aspects of the poem:

The leading character is quite uncongenial and a person who, being
made the medium of the social and other views, deprives them of
all value in fact, though to be sure you know they're Tennyson's, or
rather that Tennyson has written so about them, for as for impressing
one with sincerity, they read much more like a sort of thing the
writer thinks 'ought' to be written, but about which he feels lazy
and thinks it (as some of his readers perhaps do) nothing but a bore.[1]

In 1849 Rossetti was willing to use a Tennysonian phrase,
though it cut across the grain of his own temperament
but, when in 1855 he wrote the passage just quoted, he
turned the tables and read Tennyson in terms of his own
predispositions. The rest of the remarks on Tennyson in

[1] *Letters*, i, p. 267.

the letter (which is addressed to the Irish poet, William Allingham) are further evidence of this. Rossetti comments generally on the newly published volume which on the whole he finds disappointing. But he likes the closing lines of 'the little bit called *Will*' and finds Tennyson's truest tone in them. The poem begins 'O well for him whose will is strong' and for most of its two stanzas it is a very explicit piece of moral commentary. Stanza two describes the weak man who fails to exert his will against temptation and the concluding lines, which Rossetti liked, read:

> He seems as one whose footsteps halt,
> Toiling in immeasurable sand,
> And o'er a weary sultry land,
> Far beneath a blazing vault,
> Sown in a wrinkle of the monstrous hill,
> The city sparkles like a grain of salt.

Here emerges with striking effect the visionary Tennyson, the mystic of the Lincolnshire wolds whom Harold Nicolson endeavoured to disengage from his alter ego, the Victorian poet-laureate who held and wrote about 'social and other views' and did not shrink from being didactic. The operation risks killing the poet, for Tennyson never forgot the lesson of public responsibility which 'The Palace of Art' inculcated and Rossetti himself accepted the doctrine though he was 'bored' by what he thought of as Tennyson's over-literal application of it.

As the lives and careers of the two men developed after 'The Palace of Art' and 'Hand and Soul', their views of art diverged more and more widely but, no matter how differently he interpreted it, the older Rossetti as well as the young one shared the Victorian sense of the moral responsibility of the artist. Defending his practice against Buchanan's charges in 1871, he directs attention to three sonnets in *The House of Life* called 'The Choice' (nos. LXXI, LXXII, LXXIII) which, he says, 'sum up the general view taken' in relation to 'the responsibilities and higher mysteries of life'.[1] The sonnets are early, belonging like the three on 'Old and New Art', to the years 1848–9. They share with the poems on art a strong moralistic character. Like the others, their final message is an exhortation to be up and doing. The shadow of death hanging over all men may invite us to eat, drink and be merry for tomorrow we die or, as the second sonnet suggests, we may be so overcome with a sense of sin that we pass our lives immobilised by fear of the hereafter. The third poem presents death as a stimulus to high endeavour and the image of the sestet gives eloquent expression to a mid-nineteenth-century vista of limitless progress to which it is every individual's duty to contribute the best he has. It may have been disingenuous of Rossetti to claim in 1871 that he thought precisely as he had done in 1848, but essentially he was justified in asserting his respect, as poet, for the moral codes of society. The furthest he will go in revisionism is to confess:

That I may . . . take a wider view than some poets or critics of how much, in the material conditions absolutely given to man to deal with as distinct from his spiritual aspirations, is admissible within the limits of Art, – this, I say, is possible enough; nor do I wish to shrink from such responsibility. But to state that I do so to the ignoring or overshadowing of spiritual beauty is an absolute falsehood.[2]

The whole tone of *The Stealthy School of Criticism* is quite different from that of Swinburne and the aesthetic movement.

Rossetti's reference to the three sonnets called 'The Choice', with their theme of life lived under the shadow of death, may, in fact, have been more pointed than it at first seems. In 1868, three years earlier, Walter Pater had written a review of William Morris. He takes the same theme as Rossetti in his sonnets and the language he

[1] *Works*, i, p. 482.
[2] *Works*, i, pp. 485–6.

applies to it becomes the vocabulary of aestheticism:

we are all condamnés, as Hugo somewhere says: we have an interval
and then we cease to be. Some spend this interval in listlessness,
some in high passions, the wisest in art and song. For our chance is
in expanding that interval, in getting as many pulsations as possible
into the given time. High passions give one this quickened sense of
life . . . Of this wisdom, the poetic passion, the desire of beauty, the
love of art for art's sake, has most; for art comes to you professing
frankly to give nothing but the highest quality to your moments as
they pass, and simply for the moment's sake.[1]

Rossetti's 'Choice' poems are much more orthodox than
this. In selecting them for special mention in his reply to
Buchanan, he may have recalled Pater and expected
others to do so. He meant, at any rate, deliberately to
dissociate himself from the a-moral cult of art for art's
sake.

Pater goes on to stress, even more emphatically, the
importance of extracting the most from the moments as
they pass:

Not to discriminate every moment some passionate attitude in
those about us, and in the very brilliancy of their gifts some tragic
dividing of forces on their ways, is, on this short day of frost and
sun, to sleep before evening. With this sense of the splendour of our
experience and of its awful brevity, gathering all we are into one
desperate effort to see and touch, we shall hardly have time to make
theories about the things we see and touch. What we have to do is
to be for ever curiously testing new opinions and courting new
impressions.[2]

Rossetti also, particularly in his sonnet sequence *The
House of Life*, laid stress on the moment but his attitude
is again non-Paterean and, as with his view of the moral
responsibility of art, his thinking is closer to the general
run of mid-Victorian interests than might be supposed.

'A sonnet is a moment's monument', the prefatory
sonnet to *The House of Life* begins:

[1] *Westminster Review*, 34, November 1868, pp. 300–12.
[2] Pater reworked parts of the Morris review, including the passages
quoted, for use in the concluding chapter of *The Renaissance*.

Memorial from the soul's eternity
To one dead deathless hour. Look that it be,
Whether for lustral rite or dire portent,
Of its own arduous fulness reverent:
Carve it in ivory or in ebony,
As Day or Night may rule; and let Time see
Its flowering crest impearled and orient.

A sonnet is a coin: its face reveals
The soul, – its converse to what Power 'tis due:
Whether for tribute to the august appeals
Of Life, or dower in Love's high retinue,
It serve; or, 'mid the dark wharf's cavernous breath,
In Charon's palm it pay the toll to Death.

The 'arduous fulness' desired for sonnet and moment recalls Pater but the quality of Paterean intensity is modified by contact with deep-rooted elements in Rossetti's own mind. The 'dead deathless hour' which poetry commemorates is linked with such experiences as the quasi-mystical vision of the lover in the early poem 'The Portrait' and far from Rossetti cultivating 'the moments as they pass...simply for the moments' sake', he cherishes them for what they signify. A sonnet 'reveals The soul' and its range of reference is to love, life and death. There is nothing here of Pater's self-justifying connoisseurship of sensation, 'curiously testing new opinions and courting new impressions', that doctrine which he had second thoughts about when he withdrew the 'Conclusion' from the second edition of *The Renaissance*, lest 'it might possibly mislead some of those young men into whose hands it might fall'. On the contrary, the earnestness of purpose and the scope promised for *The House of Life* link it closely with Tennyson again, and invite comparison with *In Memoriam*.

Rossetti made a number of remarks about his sonnet-sequence which indicate clearly the scope of his ambitions for it. He wished to put in action, he said, 'a complete dramatis personae of the soul'.[1] In *The Stealthy School of*

[1] *Letters*, ii, p. 850.

Criticism (written before the final, complete version of the sequence), he referred to 'the analysis of passion and feeling attempted in *The House of Life*'[1] and the manuscript of the sonnets in the Fitzwilliam Museum, Cambridge, contains a note that the life dealt with in the sequence would be 'life representative, as associated with love and death, with aspiration and foreboding, or with ideal art and beauty'. The truth is that Rossetti was interested not simply in recording but also in interpreting his experience and in doing so he was not so detached from the intellectual ferment of his century as he sometimes liked to pretend. William Michael, his brother, said that he was 'superstitious in grain and anti-scientific to the marrow'[2] and he is alleged to have asked one day: 'What can it possibly matter whether the sun moves round the earth or the earth moves round the sun?'[3] This is in the spirit of Burne-Jones's defiant assertion: 'The more materialistic science becomes, the more angels I will paint', and for Rossetti the question was a polemical gesture rather than sober profession. He was by no means so ignorant, or so foolish, as to fail to see that what science, especially contemporary science, had to say *did* matter very much. It is ironic, all the same, that his second baptismal name should have come from Charles Lyell, father of the geologist whose work, *Principles of Geology*, antedated Darwin's *The Origin of Species* and caused a considerable stir – the young Tennyson at Cambridge sent for a copy of the book at once.

The impact of new science left a deep bruise on Tennyson and *In Memoriam* is his most extended attempt to find a salve. *The House of Life* is Rossetti's comparable statement about the findings of his own life but it may appear to be an entirely idiosyncratic one, divorced from the intellectual and emotional agitations, not of Tennyson

---

[1] *Works*, i, p. 486.
[2] Ibid., p. xxi.
[3] Graham Hough, *The Last Romantics* (London, 1949), p. 47.

alone, but of Browning and Matthew Arnold, to say nothing of the numbers of thinking men and women for whom poets and other writers found a voice. Yet the appearance of remoteness which Rossetti may give is, at least to some extent, deceptive. The view that art can be brought to the bar of moral judgement and the ambition to make a commentary on life and love and death put Rossetti in the Victorian mainstream. Some of the pressures which he felt in constructing his philosophy – not all – are identifiable with the major concerns of others. There is, for example, a late sonnet in *The House of Life* called 'The Trees of the Garden' (no. LXXXIX, 1875):

> Ye who have passed Death's haggard hills; and ye
> Whom trees that knew your sires shall cease to know
> And still stand silent: is it all a show, –
> A wisp that laughs upon the wall? – decree
> Of some inexorable supremacy
> Which ever, as man strains his blind surmise
> From depth to ominous depth, looks past his eyes,
> Sphinx-faced with unabashed augury?
>
> Nay, rather question the Earth's self. Invoke
> The storm-felled forest-trees moss-grown to-day
> Whose roots are hillocks where the children play;
> Or ask the silver sapling 'neath what yoke
> Those stars, his spray-crown's clustering gems, shall wage
> Their journey still when his boughs shrink with age.

At one time Rossetti intended the lyric called 'A Young Fir-Wood' to be included in *The House of Life* and it makes the same point as the sonnet. Both breathe a sense of the vast and inhuman expanses of time in which stands, minute, the single life, an awareness which early-nineteenth-century developments in geology, in particular, brought to bear with agonising force on contemporaries. Rossetti's questions 'is it all a show, – A wisp that laughs upon the wall?' have their counterpart in sections LIV and LV of *In Memoriam* and the fear that haunts Tennyson, of individual extinction in death, finds expression too in

The House of Life. The threat to love posed by death haunted Tennyson from an early age and the death of Arthur Hallam only precipitated a mixture of ideas and emotions which had been present in his mind for years before. 'Love and Death', 'The Deserted House' and 'Oriana' are early poems but they foreshadow the anguish, the resistance, and ultimately, the attempts to accommodate the situation, which are to be expressed in *In Memoriam.* Psychological patterns were formed early in Rossetti's life too and determined the response he made to experiences which came after. The love and death antithesis takes a different form for him but, like Tennyson, he speculates about life after death. His speculations have a distinctive cast.

When Tennyson began to write *In Memoriam* his love for Hallam seemed to him the best part of his life and the most dreaded sting of death was the threat of extinction, obliterating all human value, including this most cherished friendship. This dread leads Tennyson to ponder on the problems of immortality and possible solutions to them. He considers the hypothesis that at death all souls merge in a 'general soul' (XLVII) but rejects it for its sacrifice of individuality. Rossetti makes a comment which bears on this in a letter to Bell Scott of 1871: 'I cannot suppose that any particle of life is *extinguished,* though its permanent individuality may be more questionable.' The sentence which follows develops the train of thought on a quite different line from Tennyson's: 'Absorption is not annihilation; and it is even a real retributive future for the special atom of life to be re-embodied (if so it were) in a world which its own former ideality had helped to fashion for pain or pleasure.'[1] The idea of reincarnation which he refers to here had a considerable hold on Rossetti's imagination for it crops up throughout his

[1] *Letters,* iii, pp. 989–90. W. M. Rossetti, quoting this in his *Dante Gabriel Rossetti: Letters and Memoir,* i, p. 422, prints 'identity' for 'ideality' which he thinks is 'surely . . . a mistake'.

life. In 'Sudden Light', a poem written in 1853–4 and originally intended for *The House of Life*, his speculation has an optimistic turn:

> I have been here before,
> But when or how I cannot tell:
> I know the grass beyond the door,
> The sweet keen smell,
> The sighing sound, the lights around the shore.
>
> You have been mine before, –
> How long ago I may not know:
> But just when at that swallow's soar
> Your neck turned so,
> Some veil did fall, – I knew it all of yore.
>
> Has this been thus before?
> And shall not thus time's eddying flight
> Still with our lives our love restore
> In death's despite,
> And day and night yield one delight the more?

Pre-existence features again in a sonnet which Rossetti wrote about the same time, called 'The Birth Bond' (*The House of Life*, no. xv) and the idea of recurrent lives is behind the second stanza of 'The Cloud Confines' (written in 1871) which at one stage was intended to close *The House of Life*:

> The Past is over and fled;
> Named new, we name it the old;
> Thereof some tale hath been told,
> But no word comes from the dead;
> Whether at all they be,
> Or whether as bond or free,
> Or whether they too were we,
> Or by what spell they have sped.
> Still we say as we go, –
> Strange to think by the way,
> Whatever there is to know,
> That shall we know one day.[1]

[1] The idea of a revelation to come some day evidently fascinated Rossetti. He uses it in the sestet of his sonnet on Shelley when, writing of the fatal voyage in the mists of the gulf of Spezia, he asks:

'Whether they too were we': whether, that is, what was once called new and is now called old is, in fact, the same as our present, a life-cycle perpetually turning. The story, *Saint Agnes of Intercession*, written when Rossetti was twenty, gives the fullest development of the idea of successive lives. In the story the first person narrator, a painter, tells of his discovery that in a portrait of his fiancée he has reproduced exactly the features of a Saint Agnes painted by a fifteenth-century Italian artist who had taken *his* beloved as his model. When he finds a self-portrait of the Italian, he realises that it is a picture of himself: 'That it *was* my portrait – that the St. Agnes was the portrait of Mary, – and that both had been painted by myself four hundred years ago, – this now rose up distinctly before me as the one and only solution of so startling a mystery.'[1] Twenty years after the unfinished *Saint Agnes of Intercession*, the idea of reincarnation provided an image in the second of a group of sonnets called 'Willowwood' (*House of Life* no. L, 1868):

> And now Love sang: but his was such a song
> So meshed with half-remembrance hard to free,
> As souls disused in death's sterility
> May sing when the new birthday tarries long.[2]

Like many other of the deep-rooted ideas in Rossetti's imagination, this of reincarnation is double-faced. In 'Sudden Light' successive lives guarantee the survival of

---

> When that mist cleared, O Shelley! what dread veil
> Was rent for thee, to whom far-darkling Truth
> Reigned sovereign guide through thy brief ageless youth?
> Was the Truth *thy* Truth, Shelley? . . .

The original source may well have been canto xx of Dante's *Paradiso* where the formula 'ora conosce' (now he knows) recurs to great effect.

[1] *Works*, i, 417.

[2] P. F. Baum's explanation of the lines may be helpful: 'the idea that between successive incarnations on this planet or others, souls must wait through a "sterile" interval of greater or lesser duration. In this period they are "disused"' (*The House of Life* edited by P. F. Baum (Cambridge, Mass., 1928), p. 140).

love and they may authenticate deeply-felt affinities, as
'The Birth-Bond' suggests, but the cycle of incarnation
has also a grimmer aspect. The narrator of *Saint Agnes of
Intercession* realises this in a vision of horror: 'for the first
time I wished to die; and then it was that there came
distinctly, such as it may never have come to any other
man, the unutterable suspicion of the vanity of death'.[1]
The same vision receives powerful expression in sonnet
LXXXVI of *The House of Life*, written in 1862:

> The lost days of my life until to-day,
> What were they, could I see them on the street
> Lie as they fell? Would they be ears of wheat
> Sown once for food but trodden into clay?
> Or golden coins squandered and still to pay?
> Or drops of blood dabbling the guilty feet?
> Or such spilt water as in dreams must cheat
> The undying throats of Hell, athirst alway?
>
> I do not see them here; but after death
> God knows I know the faces I shall see,
> Each one a murdered self, with low last breath
> 'I am thyself, – what hast thou done to me?'
> 'And I – and I – thyself,' (lo! each one saith,)
> 'And thou thyself to all eternity!'[2]

'thou thyself to all eternity': in a repeated cycle of existence individuality will not be something to be cherished,
but to be oneself will be to be in hell. We may be bound
for all eternity to perpetual encounter with our own lost
days.

Rossetti's speculations move a long way from Tennyson's accustomed paths but they touch Victorian preoccupations at another point. The questions at the heart
of 'The Trees of the Garden' and of Rossetti's imagining
of reincarnation are questions not about the nature of
God, as Tennyson's tend to be, but about another

[1] *Works*, i, p. 424.
[2] I have retained the punctuation of line 11 as printed by W. M. Rossetti
and by Oswald Doughty (London, 1961) but I strongly suspect that
there should be a full stop after 'self' and a comma after 'breath'.

nineteenth-century theme, the nature of time. Discoveries about the long evolutionary process and about the ancient history of the earth stimulated the Victorian sense of time to an unprecedented degree. One consequence was the impetus given to antiquarian studies and Rossetti reflects this interest in the remote past and in distant cultures in his poem 'The Burden of Nineveh' which, like so many others, he first wrote in 1848/9 and afterwards revised.

'The Burden of Nineveh' is a remarkably accomplished poem. It consists of twenty ten-line stanzas, rhymed aaaabccccb. The b rhymes are the same throughout as each stanza ends with the word 'Nineveh'. It is a considerable feat to sustain this pattern and Rossetti does it, with one or two weaker patches, very successfully. The poem tells of a visit to the British Museum to look at the Elgin marbles. As Rossetti is leaving, porters are hoisting in through the doors 'A winged beast from Nineveh', a prize from the excavations conducted by Lanyard in 1845–6. This 'mummy of a buried faith' stands revealed in the light, and the sight of it draws Rossetti's mind back through time:

> The print of its first rush-wrapping
> Wound ere it dried, still ribbed the thing.
> What song did the brown maidens sing,
> From purple mouths alternating,
> When that was woven languidly?

The 'poor god' must now take his place in the museum galleries as an object in a history lesson on dead civilisations for school children:

> Greece, Egypt, Rome – did any god
> Before whose feet men knelt unshod
> Deem that in this unblest abode
> Another scarce more unknown god
> Should house with him, from Nineveh?

The beast from Nineveh opens a long historical perspective. Once Nineveh was in its prime but after it fell its god lay obscurely buried in the sands of the desert 'while older grew By ages the old earth and sea'. The earth and sea, old when Nineveh was young, yet remain and so does the sun. In the sunlight the shadow of the god from Nineveh falls on to the London pavements as once it fell, perhaps, on Sennacherib and Semiramis. On the day which the Bible records, when Jonah sheltered beneath the gourd outside the gates of the city, '*this* sun' shining in Malet Street in 1849 threw '*this* shadow'.

Rossetti is not concerned simply to dizzy the imagination by these vistas. Two-thirds of the way through the poem he makes a break – 'Here woke my thought.' Having immersed himself in the past, he awakes to the present. The past which his imagination has revived for a moment lapses back through the ages and the London wind sweeps away the shadow which the sun had given:

> . . . The wind's slow sway
> Had waxed; and like the human play
> Of scorn that smiling spreads away,
> The sunshine shivered off the day:
> The callous wind, it seemed to me,
> Swept up the shadow from the ground.

The image is a telling one. Under the influence of this chilly wind, Rossetti sees swept away, not only the shade of Nineveh, but also the crowd on the London pavement and the whole civilisation of which it is part. In the vast reaches of time to come, London may be as remote as Nineveh and

> . . . some may question which was first,
> Of London or of Nineveh.

Tennyson wrote of the stars as

> . . . cold fires
> Yet with power to burn and brand
> His nothingness into man.

Hall Caine included a sonnet of Rossetti's friend, William Bell Scott, in his *Sonnets of Three Centuries* (1882), called

'The Universe Void' which spoke of man 'Gasping, lost and terrified' amid the

> Revolving worlds, revolving systems, yea,
> Revolving firmaments . . .

revealed by contemporary science. Though Rossetti proclaimed his indifference to science, 'The Burden of Nineveh' is, in fact, a very contemporary poem and it gives a brilliantly imaginative treatment to a theme much handled in Victorian literature, the diminishment of man in a universe whose time and space the new learning had so fearfully enlarged.

> Time like an ever-rolling stream
> Bears all its sons away –

so Isaac Watts put it in 1719 and the Victorians had better cause to know that a thousand ages in the vast unfolding of history is but an evening gone. The hymn invokes the God of past and future and His eternal care but Rossetti's latter-day poem offers no such shelter. Not only are the differences between civilisations obliterated by time (which was first, London or Nineveh?) but so, he suggests, are the differences between gods. The gods of Greece and Egypt and Rome whom men once worshipped now stand together, dead, in the 'unblest abode' of the British Museum. As in the past, so it may be in the future. One day it may be lost to knowledge that nineteenth-century London worshipped the Christian God and it may be supposed that the winged beast of Nineveh was, in fact, the object of their reverence. A final sting is reserved for the last stanza. It is laughable that modern man should worship such an idol – or is it?

> . . . These heavy wings spread high,
> So sure of flight, which do not fly;
> That set gaze never on the sky;
> Those scriptured flanks it cannot see;
> Its crown, a brow-contracting load;
> Its planted feet which trust the sod:

(So grew the image as I trod:)
O Nineveh, was this thy God –
Thine also, mighty Nineveh?

The poem is in part a product of the broadened historical knowledge of the period and the growth of antiquarian interests. It derives some of its point from the knowledge of the incalculable ages of the world that science was forcing upon men. Archbishop Ussher in the seventeenth century had calculated the age of the earth as 6,000 years, a life-span which the mind could contemplate with relative ease, but now men found themselves instead in a 'boundless universe' of time and space. Yet 'The Burden of Nineveh' is not a cry of anguish like, for example, Arnold's 'Dover Beach'. As it reveals itself in the end, its main point is satirical. The poem attacks the pride and complacency of mid-century Britain, reducing its pretentiousness by the scale of history, and it comments on the materialism and hypocrisy of contemporary religion. The nation may claim to walk in 'Christ's lowly ways' but the god it worships has in fact as little spirituality and is as earth-bound as the god of Nineveh.

Like the laments about man's lost security in the universe, attacks on the complacency of middle-class society and on the coarseness of its religious life are common coinage in the middle of the century. Rossetti's treatment of these themes has a wit and a finesse not easily matched although the comments he makes or implies do not cut very deep. Out of the range of topical concerns which the poem includes, the one that stimulates Rossetti to his best writing is the theme of the mystery of time. It is in the service of this that the potent images are evoked, of the brown maidens at their work long ago, of the sunshine, and of the shadow which the wind sweeps up. Time engaged Rossetti's imagination very deeply. At this point his concerns and those of his contemporaries most closely mesh, though the extent to

C

which his imagination is engaged ensures that the expression he gives to his treatment of it is imbued with the marks of his own special sensibility.

The image of the shadow is especially fine in 'The Burden of Nineveh'. Perhaps Hardy was struck by it for a similar image is used for similar effect in *Tess of the d'Urbervilles*, chapter 16. That of a civilisation and its faith a shadow alone should endure is a piercing blow to man's vainglory and the shadow of the milkmaids in *Tess* makes an equally ironic comment on human pretensions. The cows are coming in to be milked and Tess follows them:

Long thatched sheds stretched round the enclosure, their slopes encrusted with vivid, green moss, and their eaves supported by wooden posts rubbed to a glossy smoothness by the flanks of infinite cows and calves of bygone years, now passed into an oblivion almost inconceivable in its profundity. Between the posts were ranged the milchers, each exhibiting herself at the present moment to a whimsical eye in the rear as a circle on two stalks, down the centre of which a switch moved pendulum-wise; while the sun, lowering itself behind this patient row, threw their shadows accurately inwards upon the wall. Thus it threw shadows of these obscure and homely figures every evening with as much care over each contour as if it had been the profile of a Court beauty on a palace wall; copied them as diligently as it had copied Olympian shapes on marble façades long ago, or the outline of Alexander, Caesar, and the Pharaohs.

This passage gives splendid imaginative expression to Hardy's sense of the vast impersonality of time which submerges the individual life, whether of cows or men, and the comments about the shadows on the wall embody Hardy's ineluctable awareness of the crucial disparity between the experience of man and the universe which surrounds him. Man creates art and history but all his creations die: the sun shines on through all the ages, totally indifferent to the distinctions made by men between the humble and the great, between to-day and a thousand years ago. These shadows in Rossetti's poem and in Hardy's novel have their origins in scientific

enlightenment but they owe their sharp and telling
definition to Hardy's pessimism and the hard-edged
scepticism which Rossetti at times exhibited. The poetic
power of Rossetti's treatment speaks for itself, whether
or not Hardy's is directly indebted to him.

The House of Life has time as a central theme, for the
common term in the titles of the two parts is 'change'.
Part one is entitled 'Youth and Change', part two
'Change and Fate' and change is the essence of time. One
sonnet in the sequence is of particular interest in the
context of the present discussion, no. LXIII called
'Inclusiveness' (1869):

> The changing guests, each in a different mood,
> Sit at the roadside table and arise:
> And every life among them in likewise
> Is a soul's board set daily with new food.
> What man has bent o'er his son's sleep, to brood
> How that face shall watch his when cold it lies? –
> Or thought, as his own mother kissed his eyes,
> Of what her kiss was when his father wooed?

> May not this ancient room thou sitt'st in dwell
> In separate living souls for joy or pain?
> Nay, all its corners may be painted plain
> Where Heaven shows pictures of some life spent well;
> And may be stamped, a memory all in vain,
> Upon the sight of lidless eyes in Hell.

It is easy to dismiss the octave as the work of a morbid
imagination but, set the lines against the background of
Rossetti's absorbing interest in time, and they look rather
different. The grip of time on Rossetti's imagination has
already been illustrated and there is ample additional
evidence. Time may be repeated in reincarnation or it
may be overcome in some dimension beyond life perceived in mystic vision. It may be arrested in a painting.
The sonnet 'For a Venetian Pastoral by Giorgione'
celebrates one such painting. The poem ends:

> . . . Be it as it was, –
> Life touching lips with immortality

the last line of which, as Rossetti expounded it to his brother: 'gives . . . the momentary contact with the immortal which results from sensuous culmination and is always a half-conscious element of it'.[1] But, these esoteric ideas apart, Rossetti was most deeply conscious of the pastness of the past. An early sonnet, 'Dawn on the Night Journey', is full of an awed sense of the inexorable passage of the present hour into the 'irrevocable Past'. William Michael Rossetti preserves among 'Versicles and Fragments' the moving lines:

> As much as in a hundred years, she's dead:
> Yet is to-day the day on which she died.

Against such a background as 'The Burden of Nineveh' and these other works provide, 'Inclusiveness' can be seen to bring together in violent conjunction what is and what, equally real, was and will be. The octave insists on change and variation. People of different temperaments and moods come and go in the continually dissolving and reforming scene of life but the fluidity of experience does not end there. Each individual is himself continually being remade in his lifetime, as circumstances force one transformation after another on him. Thus the strong young man becomes the dead old one and the woman whom the son knows only as mother was once a young girl desired and wooed by her lover. 'Où sont les neiges d'antan?' – given his sense of the power and the mystery of time it is hardly surprising that Rossetti made a celebrated translation of Villon's 'Ballad of Dead Ladies'.

The fluidity of experience is the theme, then, of the octave and it rings changes on the theme of time; but 'Inclusiveness' goes further and the sestet embodies a remarkable anticipation of later thinking. In his essay 'Does "Consciousness" Exist?' (first published in 1904) the philosopher William James illustrates by reference to

[1] *Letters*, ii, p. 727.

a room his point that experience has both mental and physical dimensions. The room in which someone sits exists both as a physical entity and as part of the person's consciousness. The 'pure experience' of the room is 'a place of intersection of two processes', one of which is connected with the inmate's biography, the other with the history of the house in which the room is. In relation to the personal biography, experience of the room 'is the last term of a train of sensations, emotions, decisions, movements, classifications, expectations etc., ending in the present, and the first term of a series of similar "inner" operations extending into the future . . . ' The physical past and future of the room, on the other hand, exist in different terms altogether and relate to such things as its furnishing in the past and its prospective destruction on some day in the future. The sestet of Rossetti's poem makes the same point by means of the same image. The identical room − 'ancient' because its physical reality has already endured beyond a number of lifetimes − may exist quite differently in diverse individual consciousnesses. In a characteristic projection from the fluidity of life's moments to the fixity of final judgement, Rossetti suggests that the room may linger in the souls of the dead as an emblem of a lifetime's virtue or a lifetime's sin. Malcolm Bradbury and James McFarlane point out the centrality of the room image to the Naturalists: 'By "removing the fourth wall" (to use the standard idiom of their practice), they had opened up a range of domestic interiors, areas of social and familial tension within which had been played out those terrible conflicts that so preoccupied the late nineteenth century. . . '[1] But naturalism was soon to be attacked by interest in another kind of interior, the interior of the mind or soul to whose exploration William James gave a powerful impetus. Rossetti makes the room itself part of the interior world. He

---

[1] *Modernism*, edited by Malcolm Bradbury and James McFarlane (Harmondsworth, 1976), pp. 195–6.

understood intuitively, before philosophy formulated it, that physical experience, even of a room, is malleable to the individual mind. 'Experience', James wrote, 'is remoulding us every moment, and our mental reaction on every given thing is really a resultant of our experience of the whole world up to that date'. This might serve as a commentary, not only on 'Inclusiveness', but on much of Rossetti's poetry. 'Given things' are commonly invested by Rossetti with the aura which is a resultant of his total experience up to that date. He gazed into what James christened 'the stream of thought, of conscious-ness, or of subjective life'[1] and developed, before the modernists, a technique of symbol and image to depict what he saw there. This will be discussed more fully in the next chapter and meanwhile we note the evidence that Rossetti was not only thoroughly aware of major preoccupations of his contemporaries and reflected them in his poetry but also that he was capable on occasion of interpreting ideas in ways which were in advance of his time. So, in 'Inclusiveness', the octave constitutes one of his renderings of the Victorian theme of time and the sestet follows it up with a remarkable attempt to push out into unexplored regions of consciousness. The kind of psychological penetration the poem represents, not into the experience of one particularised person but into the processes of mind itself, is not rare in his poetry and in considering it, we find an American predecessor who certainly influenced Rossetti.

If William James could have learnt something from Rossetti, Rossetti could and did learn from Poe. Elizabeth Barrett Browning wrote to the author that his poem 'The Raven' had produced a sensation in England[2] and, though she confided to R. H. Horne that 'it does not appear to me the natural expression of a sane intellect in whatever mood', she also added her genuine opinion that

[1] Quoted in *William James*, by Lloyd Morris (London, 1950) p. 17.
[2] Sidney P. Moss, *Poe's Major Crisis* (Durham, N.C., 1970), pp. 23–4.

'there is uncommon force and effect in the poem'.[1] The poem impressed Rossetti too and an original impulse of 'The Blessed Damozel' was a wish to make a companion piece. Poe had treated the subject of lovers parted by death from the point of view of the bereaved man, left alone on earth, and Rossetti wished to bring into focus the girl in heaven, longing for her still-living lover. It is difficult to read 'The Raven' now with entire seriousness but Poe's essay on 'The Philosophy of Composition' may induce a due critical sobriety. The essay purports to give an account of how Poe wrote the poem and there are several points in it which are likely to have caught Rossetti's attention. He discusses the use of a refrain, for example:

I resolved to diversify, and so heighten, the effect by adhering, in general, to the monotone of sound, while I continually varied that of thought: that is to say, I determined to produce continuously novel effects, by the variation of the *application* of the *refrain* – the *refrain* itself remaining, for the most part, unvaried.[2]

Rossetti's adaptation of this scheme is best seen in the ballad 'Sister Helen' which Buchanan chose to attack because of the monotony of the burden (refrain) 'repeated with little or no alteration through thirty-four verses'. Rossetti replied with contempt that 'the fact is, that the alteration of it in every verse is the very scheme of the poem'.[3]

Poe details one by one his decisions about 'The Raven'. Having determined that its tone should be melancholy, he then asks himself, 'Of all melancholy topics, what... is the *most* melancholy?' and, after that, 'when... is the most melancholy of topics most poetical?' His answers are that 'the death... of a beautiful woman is, unquestionably, the most poetical topic in the world – and equally is it beyond doubt that the lips best suited for such topic

[1] Quoted in *The Raven*, edited by J. H. Ingram (London, 1885), pp. 28–9.
[2] *Works of Edgar A. Poe* (London, 1896), v, p. 164.
[3] *Works*, i, p. 487.

are those of a bereaved lover'.[1] How far this chimes with
Rossetti, from the earliest version of 'The Portrait' on, is
obvious.

But the most interesting aspect of Poe's influence on
Rossetti is different from such matters as these. For what
'The Philosophy of Composition' makes clear about 'The
Raven' is that the poem traces the process of creation of a
symbol. Poe expounds the idea in his essay. For the most
part, he claims, the events of the poem are accountable in
naturalistic terms. The bird flies in to escape rough
weather. It has been previously taught to speak but
knows one word only. The scholar, at first amused,
becomes emotionally involved in the situation and,
'impelled... by the human thirst for self-torture, and in
part by superstition', questions the bird in such a way as
to ensure that 'Nevermore' becomes a more and more
significant and doom-laden response. Finally, Poe says,
he added the element of what he calls 'suggestiveness' in
the two final stanzas: 'The reader begins now to regard
the Raven as emblematical – but it is not until the very
last line of the very last stanza, that the intention of
making him emblematical of *Mournful and Never-ending
Remembrance* is permitted distinctly to be seen.'[2] In effect,
the poem develops through three stages according to
this account: one, the event of the raven's entry into the
house and its power of speech; two, the impact this makes
on the mind of the scholar; and three, the 'emblematising'.
Stage two is the crucial one where the mind and sensibility of the man begin to play upon the situation and
transform the whole event into a terrifying supernatural
experience. The mind of the reader, as well as that of the
man in the poem, is prepared for this transformation by
the suggestions which accumulate from the first stanza
onwards. The time is midnight, the scholar reads 'quaint
and curious volumes' of occult lore, the 'dying' embers

[1] *Works of Edgar A. Poe*, v, p. 166.
[2] Ibid. p. 174.

of the fire create its 'ghost' upon the floor...and so on. These signals alert us to possible significance in the arrival of the raven long before the increasing urgency of the man's questions brings the poem to its maximum drama and excitement. By the time the third stage is reached, with its introduction of the first metaphor, 'Take thy beak from out my heart', the episode has gathered plenty of 'richness' (Poe's word) of association and the raven has been recreated, no longer a bird but a symbol, or, as Poe puts it, he is seen to be 'emblematical of Mournful and Never-ending Remembrance'.

Poe specialised in the presentation of diseased and disordered imaginations at work in people who create for themselves images which then act upon their creators with the force of events. *The Fall of the House of Usher* and *William Wilson* provide obvious examples. This is not Rossetti's territory but Poe's interest in the interaction of physical and psychic phenomena and the relation of this to the symbol and image which express inner experience lies very close to his own practice. He learnt from Poe and refined on him so that his rehandling of 'The Raven' in 'The Blessed Damozel' involves much more than a change of view-point on the original situation: it becomes an object-lesson in the art of using physical objects and events for the rendering of the inner history of the mind.

Rossetti removes the living male from the centre of the stage and places the dead girl there instead but in his treatment of both girl and lover the poem is an advanced attempt to articulate the ineffable. In describing the girl he renders an entirely non-physical situation by material images and in presenting the man he uses simple common phenomena of everyday life to mediate an experience in which physical awareness is transcended. The interplay of material and psychic is remarkable in the awareness of both lovers but, if one remembers 'The Raven', it can be seen to be especially so in the case of the man. All the length of 'The Raven' is required to turn the bird into a symbol of inner anguish and a considerable accumulation of stage properties is needed to help Poe work the trick. The time is midnight and the season of the year is 'bleak December'. The man is stationed in a room equipped with purple curtains, velvet cushions and a bust of Pallas. As has been pointed out already, the poem is heavy with hints of the supernatural from the beginning. To read 'The Blessed Damozel' with Poe's manipulation in mind is to see that in his handling of the man's situation Rossetti is as daring, if less obtrusively so, as he is in his descriptions of the dead girl. The lover does not appear till stanza four. We are told nothing directly about his location or what he is thinking. We deduce from his first words that he is in the midst of a reverie about his dead love and we pick up from references here and in stanza eleven, his next appearance, that he is out of doors, in a wood at mid-day in autumn. Rossetti is attempting to arrive at a point, a climax of inner experience, depending on contact with the supernatural, and to do it with no aid whatever from traditional supernatural machinery. In broad daylight, with no more in the way of events than the touch of falling leaves, the song of a bird and the sound of bells, he will create an experience of the supra-physical which Poe could accomplish only by extraordinary and melodramatic means. The lover's part of 'The Blessed Damozel' consists of only three stanzas and two half-lines but in those Rossetti gives the stages of a spiritual communion. 'Surely she leaned o'er me', marks the man's first uncertain sense of the girl's presence in stanza four but he rejects it:

> Nothing: the autumn fall of leaves.
> The whole year sets apace.

Later (stanza eleven), his awareness of her is stronger but still questioning:

> Ah sweet! Even now in that bird's song,
> Strove not her accents there,
> Fain to be hearkened? . . .

In stanza seventeen, doubt is lost in the intensity of the experience and he addresses the girl directly and as though he hears her voice:

> Alas! we two, we two thou say'st!

In the end he both 'sees' and 'hears' across the barrier of death and time:

> I saw her smile . . . I heard her tears.

'The Blessed Damozel' is an ambitious poem. It attempts a modern version of such a moment of communion as Dante experienced on the first anniversary of Beatrice's death and it makes a new assemblage of the elements of physical and spiritual life. It owes something to Poe's example but it embodies a far subtler understanding of how physical imagery can be used to express psychic experience. Poe and Rossetti both deal in the supernatural or paranormal because it enables them to give some account of the stranger, less analysable aspects of mental experience. The interest is in the capacities of the mind, however, not sensationalism, though as pioneers Poe and Rossetti tend to take extreme cases and push their explorations to limits. Rossetti's favourite goal in these travels into mysterious regions is a moment of communion of souls. The psychological interest which lies behind this and the kind of imagery which is used to develop it form a major part of Rossetti's achievement as a poet. The achievement is often underestimated because its character is not clearly recognised.

One last comparison in this chapter, between Rossetti's treatment of an idea and that of contemporaries with whom he shares it, will draw attention again to his psychological interests and to his imagery. Exploration of the processes of mind under one form or another of stress is a constant preoccupation of Rossetti's poetry. His big themes, time, change, love and death, are seen in relation to the experience of the inner consciousness and he sought subjects and images which would provide him with a vocabulary for the psychological phenomena he observed. One of his most admired short poems is called 'The Woodspurge' (1856):

> The wind flapped loose, the wind was still,
> Shaken out dead from tree and hill:
> I had walked on at the wind's will,
> I sat now for the wind was still.
>
> Between my knees my forehead was, –
> My lips, drawn in, said not Alas!
> My hair was over in the grass,
> My naked ears heard the day pass.
>
> My eyes, wide open, had the run
> Of some ten weeds to fix upon;
> Among those few, out of the sun,
> The woodspurge flowered, three cups in one.
>
> From perfect grief there need not be
> Wisdom or even memory:
> One thing then learnt remains to me, –
> The woodspurge has a cup of three.

The poem records a state of extreme emotional shock in which for the time being will, thought and even emotion are reduced to mere response to immediate physical stimulus: when the wind blows, the man walks; when it stops, he sits. As he lies in the grass, his field of vision is restricted to ten weeds and of these his eye rests on just one. Afterwards he can draw no lesson from the experience of that day nor even clearly recollect it but the image of the woodspurge, impressed on the brain through the eye, contains all that cannot be said and cannot even be formulated in thought. The poem is a striking one but in its perception of the importance physical detail can acquire in moments of heightened sensibility it stands alone neither in Rossetti's own work nor that of contemporaries. The details included in 'My Sister's Sleep' and the sounds that come into the sultry chamber where Aloyse tells her story to Amelotte in 'The Bride's Prelude' are obvious examples in Rossetti's work. Ruskin explained the effect when he discussed 'the careful rendering of the inferior details' in Holman Hunt's painting, *The Awakening Conscience*. Hunt's treatment of the scene, he wrote,

is based on a truer principle of the pathetic than any of the common artistical expedients of the schools. Nothing is more notable than the way in which even the most trivial objects force themselves upon the attention of a mind which has been fevered by violent and distressful excitement. They thrust themselves forward with a ghastly and unendurable distinctness, as if they would compel the sufferer to count, or measure, or learn them by heart.[1]

The use of detail was a cardinal point in Pre-Raphaelite philosophy and in their most successful pictures the painters choose scenes which can be treated as crucial events in a lifetime. The significance is conveyed by details which derive from a past preceding the moment depicted and point to a future succeeding it. Ruskin's analysis of *The Awakening Conscience* expounds the painting in such terms. Another very clear example is Arthur Hughes's *The Long Engagement*, where the lovers' initials are overgrown by ivy and the young man's complexion hints his early death. What the Pre-Raphaelites do in their dramatic paintings, Browning does in his dramatic monologues where histories of individuals open up in the detail of revealing scenes. But in 'The Woodspurge' the detail is being used not for narrative extension but for penetration into a state of mind 'fevered by violent and distressful excitement', as Ruskin puts it. The dominance of 'trivial objects' in such a condition is a perception which Browning uses in the poem 'The Lost Mistress' published in *Dramatic Lyrics* (1845) when he makes the lover receive his rejection like this:

> All's over, then: does truth sound bitter
> As one at first believes?
> Hark, 'tis the sparrow's good-night twitter
> About your cottage eaves!

[1] From a letter to *The Times*, 25 May 1854. Ruskin's letter is extensively quoted in A. I. Grieve's second publication on *The Art of Dante Gabriel Rossetti. 'Found' and The Pre-Raphaelite Modern Life Subject* (Real World Publications, Norwich, 1976) pp. 34–5.

> And the leaf-buds in the vine are woolly,
> I noticed that, to-day;
> One day more bursts them open fully –
> You know the red turns grey.

Mrs Gaskell's *Ruth* (1853) makes effective use of the idea to describe Ruth's feelings when she is abandoned by her seducer:

[Ruth] had no penitence, no consciousness of error or offence: no knowledge of any one circumstance but that he was gone. Yet afterwards – long afterwards – she remembered the exact motion of a bright green beetle busily meandering among the wild thyme near her and she recalled the musical, balanced, wavering drop of a skylark into her nest, near the heather-bed where she lay (chapter 8).

The young William Morris manages the effect less well when, in his *Story of the Unknown Church* (one of his contributions to *The Oxford and Cambridge Magazine* of 1856), he makes the narrator fix obsessively on the garden plants growing round the window of the room where his friend lies dying. George Eliot generalises, rather heavy-handedly, on Adam Bede's concentration on the clock in the passage of Mr Irvine's house: 'In our times of bitter suffering, there are almost always these pauses, when our consciousness is benumbed to everything but some trivial perception or sensation. It is as if semi-idiocy came to give us rest from the memory and the dread which refuse to leave us in our sleep.'[1]

---

[1] *Adam Bede*, published in 1859, chap. 39. Tennyson's 'Maud', written in the mid-1850s, also offers a comment:

> Strange that the mind, when fraught
> With a passion so intense
> One would think that it well
> Might drown all life in the eye, –
> That it should, by being so overwrought,
> Suddenly strike on a sharper sense
> For a shell, or a flower, little things
> Which else would have been past by!
>
> Part two, ii, viii

Hardy's 'Neutral Tones' of 1867 may owe something to 'The Wood-spurge' for there are a number of indications that Hardy retained strong impressions from a reading of Rossetti. See appendix A.

The idea was, it would seem, fairly active in the 1850s but though all the instances cited share a common perception, only Rossetti has the confidence to employ it to create a free-standing symbol. The situation in 'The Woodspurge' is left unexplained and the comment in the last stanza simply leaves us with the flower and its 'cup of three'. Here, as elsewhere, Rossetti is seeking symbols in the physical world which will carry the weight of psychological observation, and the narrative framework which others use is an irrelevance to him. It may even be an encumbrance and when on occasions he saddles himself with it the result tends to weakness. He never managed to work his way through the complicated story of 'The Bride's Prelude' and the only part of this incomplete poem which is of value is the evocation of the hot, claustrophobic chamber where innocence first becomes acquainted with guilt and evil hangs suffocatingly in the air.

Some of the intellectual interests which Rossetti shared with his contemporaries have been identified in this chapter and some points at which characteristic features of his style match with theirs. It has not enhanced his reputation in the past that he has been regarded as entirely an alien offshoot from the main branch of mid-Victorian life and literature, with interests and artistic ambitions different from those of others. This view of him needs considerable modification. Yet it has to be acknowledged that each point of contact leads to a point of difference. Ultimately, when we put Rossetti's work alongside that of his fellows, we see a kinship but we also have a clearer view of the qualities which make him individual and worth study as in himself an original and valuable poet. At the heart of the differences between him and others who use similar ideas and techniques is his continual pressure upon the apparent boundary between physical and spiritual experience. In his poetry, whether, for instance, in the sonnet 'Inclusiveness' or in 'The

Blessed Damozel', the concentration of his mind along this frontier takes the form of psychological exploration. In the service of this Rossetti needs, most essentially, a vocabulary of image and symbol. Some points relating to this have already emerged and the next chapter will take up the subject more fully.

3
The inner world

THOUGH Rossetti sometimes shared the interests and opinions of contemporaries who were temperamentally very different from himself, his vocabulary of images is a distinctive creation, fashioned to express what is most personal and original in his vision. To set off the positive argument of this chapter, it may be useful to begin with a negative demonstration by looking at a poem where Rossetti is working under another influence and where the images he adopts, powerful in the original, fail to yield their virtue to him. The poem is 'The White Ship', a late ballad, and the influence is Coleridge's. 'In the long run', William Rossetti wrote of his brother, 'he perhaps enjoyed and revered Coleridge beyond any other modern poet whatsoever'[1] and 'The White Ship' testifies to Rossetti's response to 'The Ancient Mariner'. The ballad tells of the death by drowning of Henry I's son and heir with all his company, on 25 November 1120, and, as in Coleridge's poem, the sea provides a setting in which the chief actors are confronted with the mysteries of life and death:

> The sails were set, and the oars kept tune
> To the double flight of the ship and the moon:
>
> Swifter and swifter the White Ship sped
> Till she flew as the spirit flies from the dead:
>
> And white as a lily glimmered she
> Like a ship's fair ghost upon the sea.

As in 'The Ancient Mariner', heavenly bodies are presences which seem to participate in the events: moon and ship move onwards together and the stars throng silently

[1] *Works*, i, p. xxvi.

overhead while the young and strong sing a happy song –
a song of joy which suddenly dissolves into a shriek of
terror as the ship strikes a submerged rock. Later,
Bertold the butcher, the only survivor of the princely
company, tells how he and a nobleman's son clung to a
piece of floating wreckage and how:

> . . . each knew each, as the moments sped,
> Less for one living than for one dead:

> And every still star overhead,
> Seemed an eye that knew we were but dead.

The very short stanzas are a disservice to the poem for
they halt the action too frequently but Rossetti imparts to
the story some effective and vivid touches. The scene in
which the 'lawless shameless' Prince turns back to the
doomed ship to rescue his sister, the mutual sympathy
of the butcher and the nobleman in their extremity, and
the anguish of Fitz-Stephen the pilot are all dramatically
handled. Rossetti realises very well the human drama of
the situation and he uses the presences of sun and moon
and stars effectively for its setting. But Coleridge did
something different and so also did Gerard Manley
Hopkins and Thomas Hardy when they too found in
disaster at sea a situation focusing the major fact of
human life, its confrontation with death. In 'The Wreck
of the *Deutschland*' and 'The Convergence of the Twain'
Hopkins and Hardy are stimulated to an avowal of
deeply-felt views about life and death and suffering. To
Hopkins, the wreck of the *Deutschland* is an event full
of human terror and pain but also, ultimately, an affirmation of the Christian triumph over suffering and death.
To Hardy, the sinking of the *Titanic* exemplifies the
workings of a Fate which has no care for humanity. In
the inexorable drawing together of the great proud ship
and the iceberg, human lives are crushed and extinguished
by impersonal, indifferent forces. The poems treat of
contemporary events whereas the loss of 'The White

Ship' belonged to a distant past but even so, it might, assisted by the Coleridgean imagery, have evoked from Rossetti some depth of response. This does not happen. Without either Hardy's view of the Immanent Will[1] or

[1] It has already been suggested (p. 56) that, in spite of fundamental differences in the outlook of the two men, aspects of Rossetti's imagery were congenial to Hardy. Two other examples may be noted here. The description of the ship-wreck in 'The White Ship' includes this couplet:

> To the toppling decks clave one and all
> As a fly cleaves to a chamber-wall.

The image implies the insignificance of the human beings caught helpless between sea and sky and the image occurs again in the poem 'Even So':

> But the sea stands spread
> As one wall with the flat skies,
> Where the lean black craft like flies
> Seem well-nigh stagnated,
> Soon to drop off dead.

The context is a mood in which life seems drained of interest and purpose. All that is left is 'Sand and strewn sea-weed'. All there is to wait for is the fall into nothingness. In the last stanza of 'The Cloud Confines', the merging of sea and sky again stresses the desolation of the individual consciousness amid the immensities of time and space:

> The sky leans dumb on the sea,
> Aweary with all its wings;
> And oh! the song the sea sings
> Is dark everlastingly.
> Our past is clean forgot,
> Our present is and is not,
> Our future's a sealed seedplot,
> And what betwixt them are we?

In such passages as these, Rossetti is treating a familiar and recurrent Hardyan theme. The boy Jude, scaring off the rooks from Farmer Troutham's field, stands in a place where much has happened but where the past is 'clean forgot' as every year the harrow passes over the land. Tess and Marion hack swedes at Flintcomb Ash in a similarly vacant universe:

the whole field was in colour a desolate drab; it was a complexion without features, as if a face, from chin to brow, should be only an expanse of skin. The sky wore, in another colour, the same likeness; a white vacuity of countenance with the lineaments gone. So these two upper and nether visages confronted each other all day long, the white face looking down on the brown face, and the brown face looking up at the white face, without anything standing between them but the two girls crawling over the surface of the former like flies (*Tess of the d'Urbervilles*, chapter 43).

Hopkins's religious faith, Rossetti leaves open both possibilities in his poem but the events lead to no insight of his own. The dramatic value of the story stands on its own and in the end drama itself slides off into sentiment. Rossetti responded to the power of mysterious suggestion in Coleridge's poem and adopted the more obvious properties of 'The Ancient Mariner' but he was not enabled to make a spiritual journey of his own by these means. Sun and moon and cloud and wind occur in the titles of sonnets in *The House of Life* but their value and function are very different from what they are in Coleridge's poem. The region of Rossetti's poetry is not the wide expanses of an empty world but an area deep in inner consciousness where natural forms respond in unfamiliar ways to the pressures and moods of the imagination.

A sonnet from *The House of Life* enables us to move closer to Rossetti's world. This is 'The Monochord' (no. LXXIX, 1870):

> Is it this sky's vast vault or ocean's sound
> That is Life's self and draws my life from me,
> And by instinct ineffable decree
> Holds my breath quailing on the bitter bound?
> Nay, is it Life or Death, thus thunder-crown'd,
> That 'mid the tide of all emergency
> Now notes my separate wave, and to what sea
> Its difficult eddies labour in the ground?
>
> Oh! what is this that knows the road I came,
> The flame turned cloud, the cloud returned to flame,
> The lifted shifted steeps and all the way? –
> That draws round me at last this wind-warm space,
> And in regenerate rapture turns my face
> Upon the devious coverts of dismay?

The second example is the image of fatal growth which occurs in Rossetti's 'The King's Tragedy' and in 'The Convergence of the Twain'. In 'The King's Tragedy' it takes the form of the shroud which the old woman sees in her visions gradually rising year by year to cover the figure of the doomed king. In 'The Convergence of the Twain' Hardy describes the growth, seas apart, of ship and iceberg in complementary progression, till at last they complete their fate by merging.

It is a difficult poem and it provoked some discussion between William Rossetti and Christina when he was preparing his book *Dante Gabriel Rossetti as Designer and Writer* in 1889. William found the sonnet very obscure and Christina suggested: 'don't you think the point may be the common essence (so to say) of all these outward and inward matters? – as if one thread (the musical monochord...) ran through all, vibrated through all? Thus we should get the sort of truth which the blind man so neatly conveyed who likened *scarlet* to the sound of the trumpet.' In his note on the poem in the 1911 edition of Rossetti's works, William wrote, still tentatively, that 'I understand the general purport of the sonnet to be this: There is an unspeakably mysterious bond between the universe and the soul of man (macrocosm and microcosm): The phenomena of nature search the inmost recesses of the soul, inspiring awe, administering solace.' Rossetti himself wrote that the poem had to do with 'That sublimated mood of the soul in which a separate essence of itself seems as it were to oversoar and survey it.'[1] The three comments have little in common except an agreement that the poem expresses a unity of some kind. A question about the nature of that unity may, in fact, be at the heart of the sonnet. The sestet suggests something like a tutelary spirit brooding over and directing the poet's life beneficently, bringing him at last to a haven of comfort. Rossetti's note about 'sublimation' would suit this idea but it seems less appropriate to the octave. 'The sky's vast vault' and 'the ocean's sound' are images which recur in Rossetti's work denoting respectively eternity or spiritual life, and time or material existence. The octave questions, as much of the second part of *The House of Life* questions, whether human experience is entirely

---

[1] All the comments quoted are reproduced in Doughty's *Victorian Romantic*, pp. 691–2. Doughty's own account of the sonnet is, according to his habit, remorselessly and exclusively in terms of his hypotheses about Rossetti's life.

time-bound and subject finally to death, or whether there is some further dimension beyond the grave. The second line reflects the paradox that we begin to die as soon as we are born and the whole quatrain is about the fear of death which accompanies conscious life. The second quatrain substitutes life and death for sky and sea and imagines one of them, as presiding power, noting the poet's individual life and foreseeing its destiny. In the sestet, the authority of the octave, determinative but remote, has become a kind and comforting spirit. If it were named, it would perhaps be love, for life, love and death are the trinity of the sequence. In the prefatory poem Rossetti described a sonnet as a coin and these three are the alternative powers to which it may be offered as tribute. Which of these powers is, in fact, the mono-chord, the one string on which the various notes of a lifetime are sounded? The weight of the poem is tilted towards the sympathetic spirit of the sestet and this marks a rare moment of relative security in the sequence.

If this reading of the sonnet is right, William and Christina Rossetti missed the particular point of this poem but they noticed something more important. Their comments concentrate on the fusion of what Christina calls 'outward and inward matters' and William speaks of 'an unspeakably mysterious bond between the universe and the soul of man'. Whatever Rossetti wished to express in 'The Monochord' he tried to express through images of nature and the images are familiar ones in his writing. Not only sea and sky but roads, hills, flame and coverts are prominent in his repertoire of symbols. His use of the natural world to provide images of elusive, fragile, deeply-affecting but scarcely graspable inner experiences is one of the most distinguishing marks of his poetry. His brother, commenting on assertions that Dante Gabriel cared nothing for nature, makes the evidently right observation: 'To the beauties of Nature he was not insensitive, but he was incurious, and he valued them more as being so much fuel to the fire of the soul than as being objects of separate regard and analysis.'[1] From as early as 'My Sister's Sleep' Rossetti had sought a medium in the physical world which would convey what he wanted to say. In that poem he had used 'homely externals' to bring out 'the inner soul of the subject'[2] and, though in maturity he more commonly used natural than domestic detail, he continued throughout his life to work on the basis of what he had perceived at nineteen about psychological process and poetic method – that is, that easily recognised externals can be used to bring to view prospects which would remain unseen but for some familiar medium through which to focus them.

Commentators on Rossetti's use of natural imagery often relate it to his painter's eye though, in fact, Rossetti uses natural detail more in his poems than in his paintings. The significant details in the pictorial work derive more commonly from non-natural objects, but the natural world is everywhere in the poetry. The appeal to the mind's eye may sometimes be very great, as in the sonnet 'Silent Noon' (*The House of Life*, no. xix, 1871):

> Your hands lie open in the long fresh grass –
> The finger-points look through like rosy blooms:
> Your eyes smile peace. The pasture gleams and glooms
> 'Neath billowing skies that scatter and amass.
> All round our nest, far as the eye can pass,
> Are golden kingcup-fields with silver edge
> Where the cow-parsley skirts the hawthorn-hedge.
> 'Tis visible silence, still as the hour-glass.
>
> Deep in the sun-searched growths the dragon-fly
> Hangs like a blue thread loosened from the sky: –
> So this wing'd hour is dropt to us from above.
> Oh! clasp we to our hearts, for deathless dower,
> This close-companioned inarticulate hour
> When twofold silence was the song of love.

The first two lines of the sestet, while seeming to continue

[1] *Dante Gabriel Rossetti: Letters and Memoir*, i, pp. 410–11.
[2] *Works*, i, p. 496.

and even to intensify the visual imagery, in fact make the transition to the last four in which visual description is found to be not the end but the means. The experience of perfect companionship and love is 'inarticulate' and indescribable in itself but images from the natural world enable Rossetti to express it. Donne, in 'The Ecstasy', puts his lovers out of doors on a bank of violets, but he interprets their silence not through the life of nature, but through the intellectual refinements of Leone Ebreo. In Rossetti's poem the landscape itself conveys to us 'the song of love' contained in 'twofold silence'. In the silence of the natural scene, life, vibrant and rich, fulfils itself. The lovers also experience an intensification of life, a moment in which existence is justified as an absolute value, one of those moments out of time which Rossetti sought as a 'deathless dower' to cherish through years and changes to come.

One image which is always highly evocative to Rossetti may first have taken hold of his imagination because of Guido Guinizzelli's use of it in the famous canzone which Rossetti translated:

> Al cor gentil ripara sempre Amore
> Come a la selva augello in la verdura –

> Within the gentle heart Love shelters him
> As birds within the green shade of the grove.

Once found, the image recurs early and late. At Kelmscott in 1871 Rossetti watched the behaviour of birds at sunset with special interest:

> To-night this sunset spreads two golden wings
> Cleaving the western sky;
> Winged too with wind it is, and winnowings
> Of birds; as if the day's last hour in rings
> Of strenuous flight must die.

> Sun-steeped in fire, the homeward pinions sway
> Above the dovecot-tops;
> And clouds of starlings, ere they rest with day,
> Sink, clamorous like mill-waters, at wild play,
> By turns in every copse:

Each tree heart-deep the wrangling rout receives –
Save for the whirr within,
You could not tell the starlings from the leaves;
Then one great puff of wings, and the swarm heaves
Away with all its din.

Typically the poem, 'Sunset Wings', goes on to use the natural observation for the expression of a human experience:

Even thus Hope's hours, in ever-eddying flight,
To many a refuge tend;
With the first light she laughed, and the last light
Glows round her still; who natheless in the night
At length must make an end.

And now the mustering rooks innumerable
Together sail and soar,
While for the day's death, like a tolling knell,
Unto the heart they seem to cry, Farewell,
No more, farewell, no more!

Is Hope not plumed, as 'twere a fiery dart?
And oh! thou dying day,
Even as thou goest must she too depart,
And Sorrow fold such pinions on the heart
As will not fly away?

When he wrote 'The King's Tragedy' for the 1881 volume the image made a characteristic appearance:

Then he smiled the smile I knew so well
When he thought to please the Queen;
The smile which under all bitter frowns
Of fate that rose between,
For ever dwelt at the poet's heart
Like the bird of love unseen.

The House of Life sonnets contain notable examples on a more extended scale, 'Winged Hours', for example (no. xxv, 1869), where a bird in a leafy grove leads into intimate areas of the soul:

Each hour until we meet is as a bird
That wings from far his gradual way along
The rustling covert of my soul – his song
Still loudlier trilled through leaves more deeply stirr'd:

But at the hour of meeting, a clear word
Is every note he sings, in Love's own tongue;
Yet, Love, thou know'st the sweet strain suffers wrong,
Full oft through our contending joys unheard.

What of that hour at last, when for her sake
No wing may fly to me, nor song may flow;
When, wandering round my life unleaved, I know
The bloodied feathers scattered in the brake,
And think how she, far from me, with like eyes
Sees through the untuneful bough the wingless skies?

'The rustling covert of my soul': in this spatial imagery time itself becomes a bird travelling into the recesses of the mind till it arrives at the moment of lovers' meeting. In 'Sleepless Dreams', written in the same year (no. xxxix), the grove without the bird has become a reality experienced in tormented nights:

Girt in dark growths, yet glimmering with one star,
O night desirous as the nights of youth!

. . .

Nay, night deep-leaved! And would Love feign in thee
Some shadowy palpitating grove that bears
Rest for man's eyes and music for his ears?
O lonely night! art thou not known to me,
A thicket hung with masks of mockery
And watered with the wasteful warmth of tears?

Of the recurrent images in Rossetti's work this, of the bird and the leafy grove to denote the most sensitive area of inner personal life, is the most moving and most often employed with subtle variation, but the inner landscape which his poems describe has many features and landmarks. In his chapter on Rossetti in *Appreciations*, Pater writes of 'the shadowy world, which he realises so powerfully' and points out that it not only has ways and houses, land and water, light and darkness, but also personifications such as Death, Love, Sleep presented with 'really imaginative vividness' and 'a whole "populace" of special hours and places'.[1] Pater compares these

[1] W. H. Pater, *Appreciations* (first published 1889; edition cited Edinburgh, 1931), pp. 216–17 and 221.

aspects of Rossetti's imagery with Dante but a determining influence on some characteristics of Rossetti's spatial imagery and the populace of his inner world is likely to have been Shelley. Rossetti read and admired Shelley when he was young and the two-way process of Shelley's imagery, realising the ideal and idealising the real, is relevant to his own quest after physical symbols for, in Mrs Shelley's words, 'the most delicate and abstract emotions and thoughts of the mind'. In a passage from one of his notebooks which Mrs Shelley quotes in her 'Note on *Prometheus Unbound*', Shelley comments on spatial imagery in terms which are strikingly apt to Rossetti's use of it:

In the Greek Shakespeare, Sophocles, we find the image, πολλὰς δ'ὁδοὺς ἐλθόντα φροντίδος πλάνοις: a line of almost unfathomable depth of poetry; yet how simple are the images in which it is arrayed!
'Coming to many ways in the wanderings of careful thought.'
   If the words ὁδοὺς and πλάνοις had not been used, the line might have been explained in a metaphorical instead of an absolute sense, as we say '*ways* and means' and 'wanderings' for error and confusion. But they meant literally paths or roads, such as we tread with our feet; and wanderings, such as a man makes when he loses himself in a desert, or roams from city to city . . . What a picture does this suggest of the mind as a wilderness of intricate paths, wide as the universe, which is here made its symbol; a world within a world which he who seeks some knowledge with respect to what he ought to do searches throughout, as he would search the external universe for some valued thing which was hidden from him upon its surface.

There could hardly be a better commentary on some of Rossetti's sonnets, the sestet of 'Lost on Both Sides' (no. XCI, 1854), for example:

> So separate hopes, which in a soul had wooed
> The one same Peace, strove with each other long,
> And Peace before their faces perished since:
> So through that soul, in restless brotherhood,
> They roam together now, and wind among
> Its bye-streets, knocking at the dusty inns.

Prometheus Unbound has itself a 'populace of hours', among them some which have the sculpted quality of the heavy-curled charioteer who is an emblem of Time in Rossetti's sonnet 'Retro me Sathana' (no. XC, 1847). Other figures, in Shelley and Rossetti, have more individual quality. In *Prometheus Unbound*, Act II, sc. iv, Asia describes a vision of:

> . . . cars drawn by rainbow-winged steeds
> Which trample the dim winds

and she goes on:

> . . . In each there stands
> A wild-eyed charioteer urging their flight.
> Some look behind, as fiends pursued them there,
> And yet I see no shapes but the keen stars:
> Others with burning eyes, lean forth, and drink
> With eager lips the wind of their own speed,
> As if the thing they loved fled on before,
> And now, even now, they clasped it. Their bright locks
> Stream like a comet's flashing hair . . .

(lines 130–8)

The same animistic imagination vitalises guilt and remorse in Rossetti's sonnet 'Lost Days' (quoted on p. 51) and 'The hour which might have been yet might not be' of 'Stillborn Love' (no. LV, 1870) and the 'mournful forms' of sonnet no. L. Blake was another influence in fashioning the population of the soul, as Rossetti's comments on the poem 'Broken Love' indicate: 'The speaker is one whose soul has been intensified by pain to be his only world, among the scenes, figures and events of which he moves as in a new state of being. The emotions have been quickened and isolated by conflicting torment, till each is a separate companion.'[1] Whatever the appropriateness to Blake, the description is very apt to many of Rossetti's poems.

Sonnet L belongs to a group of four which are given the separate title 'Willowwood' within *The House of Life*. They were written in 1868 and William Rossetti described them at the time as about the finest poems his brother

[1] *Works*, i, p. 462.

had yet written. Recent commentators have tended to accept a high estimation of these sonnets but they have by no means agreed on their function and meaning in the sequence. The four sonnets occur in all versions of *The House of Life* from 1869 onwards and may be reasonably supposed to belong to a central area of the experience which the sequence embodies; but attempts to relate the other sonnets structurally to this group have not so far been convincing. The identity of the woman whose face is seen in the stream – is it Elizabeth Siddal? or Jane Morris? – and the significance of the poet's drinking of the water at the end of the fourth poem are questions which have engaged special attention. William Rossetti gives some warrant for identifying the lady in the stream with Mrs Morris when he writes: 'The four sonnets named "Willowwood" represent in a general sense, the pangs of severance... By severance we might understand "severance by death", for both the word and the idea extend to that; but severance by untoward conditions on earth appears to be more particularly contemplated in the sonnets.'[1] If this hint is accepted, it may be right to connect the 'Willowwood' sonnets with nos. XLV and XLVI, 'Secret Parting' and 'Parted Love' (both 1869). As for the drinking of the stream's water in (iv), several commentators agree that it is a purgative act of some sort, though Lionel Stevenson appears not to share this view when he equates the four sonnets with Carlyle's 'centre of indifference' and takes them as 'a declaration of frustration and self-pity'.[2]

---

[1] *D. G. Rossetti as Designer and Writer* (London, 1889), p. 216.

[2] *The Pre-Raphaelite Poets* (North Carolina, 1972), p. 68. Discussions of 'Willowwood' are included in the following publications: D. J. Robillard, 'Rossetti's "Willowwood" Sonnets and the Structure of *The House of Life*', *Victorian Newsletter*, Fall 1962, pp. 5–9; W. E. Fredeman, 'Rossetti's *In Memoriam*: An Elegiac Reading of *The House of Life*', *Bulletin of the John Rylands Library*, 47, 1964–5, pp. 298–341; H. A. Talon, D. G. Rossetti '*The House of Life*': *quelques aspects de l'art, des thèmes et du symbolisme* (*Archives des lettres modernes*, 1966).

The poems present an intense concentration of typical Rossettian imagery. Since the purpose of this imagery is to make possible the expression of feeling which would otherwise be inarticulate, it is on the face of it unlikely that any key will unlock a 'meaning' which can be simply stated and contribute to biography in a conventional sense. Commentary on the progress of the images may, however, draw out some of the qualities of these outstanding poems.

The sonnets constitute a self-contained drama. In the first of them the poet, accompanied by the figure of Love, sits by a 'woodside well'. Love touches his lute and, as the poet listens, the sound of the music melts into the voice of a beloved woman. The lover weeps and Love's eyes reflected in the water change into *her* eyes and, as Love stirs the water, the ripples that it makes become her hair. The lover stoops and her mouth in the water meets his in a kiss. Such a digest of it may make the poem sound merely bizarre but this is far from being so:

> I sat with Love upon a woodside well,
> Leaning across the water, I and he;
> Nor ever did he speak nor looked at me,
> But touched his lute wherein was audible
> The certain secret thing he had to tell:
> Only our mirrored eyes met silently
> In the low wave; and that sound came to be
> The passionate voice I knew; and my tears fell.
>
> And at their fall, his eyes beneath grew hers;
> And with his foot and with his wing-feathers
> He swept the spring that watered my heart's drouth.
> Then the dark ripples spread to waving hair,
> And as I stooped, her own lips rising there
> Bubbled with brimming kisses at my mouth.[1]

---

[1] Margaret Macdonald did a panel for the Willow Tea Rooms, Sauchiehall Street, Glasgow, based on the Willowwood sonnets. The following description of it was included in the catalogue of the Charles Rennie MacKintosh (1868–1928) centenary exhibition in the Victoria and Albert Museum (catalogue compiled by Andrew McLaren Young):

The familiar image of the wood or grove indicates at once that we are in the 'world within a world'. The water of the well, 'the spring that watered my heart's drouth', is located also within this interior world. As the poet sits in grief and longing, withdrawn within the landscape of the mind, through the agency of Love he passes yet a stage further from the outer world to a point where sounds and sights dissolve and are recomposed and where an image from the depth of the soul takes on a tangible reality. In fourteen lines we have been removed several stages from the level of surface consciousness and the method used has been one of plain statement, an apparently simple record of actions performed, every movement precise, with no haziness of language or idea. The sonnet is a remarkable blend of the surrealistic with a kind of factual dispassionateness and it conditions us for the further stages in the unfolding of the drama.

In the second sonnet Love sings but what his song evokes is not joy, but disappointment, frustration and regret. The song is 'meshed with half-remembrance', for the present moment is still caught in the toils of an unhappy past. Longing and disappointment have bitten too deep for confidence to assert itself now. The image in lines 3 and 4 is drawn from the notion of reincarnation which interested Rossetti (see pp. 48–51). The lovers have experienced the sterility of death in a life without love, and hope long deferred has weakened their faith in a new birth to love triumphant and fulfilled. In the train of memory comes the 'dumb throng' of days and hours, 'mournful forms' who witness to regret and sorrow and failure:

The panel depicts the elongated form of a woman submerged to the neck in water and a kneeling man (both apparently naked) kissing her. He is *not* in the water. Large bubbles drip from the woman's left hand. Her eyes are shut, his appear to be open and there is something wolfish in the thrust forward of the head. He is all thrustful and greedy, she leans a little backwards and her lines are curved and drooping (like her breasts).

> . . . I was made aware of a dumb throng
> That stood aloof, one form by every tree,
> All mournful forms, for each was I or she,
> The shade of those our days that had no tongue.
>
> They looked on us, and knew us and were known;
> While fast together, alive from the abyss,
> Clung the soul-wrung implacable close kiss;
> And pity of self through all made broken moan
> Which said, 'For once, for once, for once alone!'

The tone of these lines is desperate. The lovers' appeal for release, if only for once, from the oppressive influence of the past weighing on present and future finds no answer in the kiss which is 'implacable' because it cannot assuage this pain.

The third poem gives the words of Love's song. It is addressed to all frustrated lovers who long in vain for a love once known and never forgotten. They walk in Willowwood, 'with hollow faces burning white', starved of the sustenance which they crave, struck, fathoms deep, in a widowhood of the soul. With Willowwood in sonnet LI, we are in the depths of the leafy covert of the soul, having moved from the 'woodside well' of the first poem of the group to the centre. This wood is a place of nightmare with 'bitter banks' and 'tear-spurge wan' and 'blood-wort burning red'. Better to die than be condemned to wander here. The willow, traditional symbol of forlorn lovers, becomes a dark and fearful part of Rossetti's soulscape, haunted with suggestions of anguish and deprivation and guilt. The complex feelings of extreme emotional tension are strongly evoked, the images gaining in power by the carefully designed rhetorical structure of the poem. The first two lines invoke the audience's attention with heavy repetition and alliteration. The next six compose one sentence, with the main verb held in suspense till line 8. The sestet ends with a couplet, an infrequent form in the sequence but appropriate here to give clinching expression to the despair of the poem.

Repetition, alliteration and internal rhyme are used throughout and the repeated *a* rhyme (on 'willowwood'), which runs all through, adds to the insistent rhythm of hopelessness:

'O ye, all ye that walk in Willowwood,
That walk with hollow faces burning white;
What fathom-depth of soul-struck widowhood,
What long, what longer hours, one lifelong night,
Ere ye again, who so in vain have wooed
Your last hope lost, who so in vain invite
Your lips to that their unforgotten food,
Ere ye, ere ye again shall see the light!

Alas! the bitter banks in Willowwood,
With tear-spurge wan, with blood-wort burning red:
Alas! if ever such a pillow could
Steep deep the soul in sleep till she were dead, –
Better all life forget her than this thing,
That Willowwood should hold her wandering!'

This poem marks the furthest point to which the group of sonnets penetrates. Their subject is longing and hopelessness and the second and third reveal in searing vision a complex of tormenting emotions. After this, in the fourth sonnet, there is a gradual return to something like common life. As Love's song dies away, so ends the meeting in the kiss. The lovers draw apart and the image now used, of roses shedding their petals at the end of day, lacks the sharp focus and metaphoric intensity of the earlier poems. The woman's face is drowned again in the water and the poet stoops and drinks and absorbs into himself 'Her breath and all her tears and all her soul', an act, it would seem, denoting inseparable identification with her. Love makes a gesture of commiseration. At the end of the octave, the lover comments on the disappearance of the woman's face:

... if it ever may
Meet mine again I know not if Love knows,

and the final lines of the sestet, in which both the lover's and Love's heads are encircled by Love's aureole, share

D

something of the detachment which belongs to comment rather than the unselfconscious immersion in experience of the central poems. The drama of the four sonnets ends with normal consciousness reasserting itself in expressions of doubt and hope as the visionary intensity fades.[1]

The function of this group of poems is not a narrative one, for *The House of Life* is not a narrative sequence. In its two-part structure, it sums up the experience of a lifetime in a series of selected significant moments. The first part deals primarily with the experience of love and, in the Willowwood sonnets, many of the strands which appear separately elsewhere gather into a knot of inter-linked emotions. Rossetti's individual manner is seen at its most daring and original in this group, for he puts all the weight on to the vocabulary of image and symbol which he has built up, and he takes the reader at once to the borders of a visionary landscape and leads him further

---

[1] The young poet, Théophile Marzials, admired Rossetti and a poem of his, evidently influenced by 'Willowwood', was included in *English Sonnets by Living Writers. Selected and Arranged, with a note on the History of the 'Sonnet'* by Samuel Waddington (London, 1881). It is called 'Love, the Intimidator' and reads like a parody:

> Beside a fountain's spurting trumpeter
> A large white-throated lady lean'd and flung
> Her long-sleeved arms above her dulcimer,
> And quick the glib notes ran along her tongue,
> Like rose and fruit. '*Ah bitter love!*' she sung;
> Then lustily: '*Sweet Death, the comforter!*'
> It chanced that Love, the garden-slopes among,
> Came like the palmer, Death, and look'd at her.

> The lady swoon'd amid her stiff brocades,
> And wept amain, though Love laugh'd low and sweet.
> She call'd on Love, but Love with rapid feet
> Pass'd out amid the sombre laurel-shades,
> Unto the chamber of her nooning maids,
> And bade them broider at her winding-sheet.

Marzials sent Rossetti a copy of his volume called *The Gallery of Pigeons* (1873) and Rossetti wrote to Ford Madox Brown: 'Have you received this *Pigeon* book by Marzials? Good God! And Scott tells me it produces exactly the same impression on him that my things did when he first saw them! I see Bob Buchanan must be in the right.' (*Letters*, iii, p. 1163).

and further in. Buchanan, like others before and since, was
unable to find the territory on any map but critical lack
of sympathy or impercipience should not permanently
obscure the remarkable extension of poetic expressiveness which Rossetti achieved in such writing as this.

The symbols and symbolic mode of the Willowwood
sonnets are closely related to another poem, written in
1869–71. 'The Stream's Secret' has the same motifs as the
sonnet group and shares the same imagery but it provides
a more explicit account of the situation which apparently
gives rise to them. Even more explicit is sonnet XL of *The
House of Life*, called 'Severed Selves' (1871). The octave
describes the separation of lovers and the sestet continues:

> Such are we now. Ah! may our hope forecast
> Indeed one hour again, when on this stream
> Of darkened love once more the light shall gleam? –
> An hour how slow to come, how quickly past, –
> Which blooms and fades, and only leaves at last,
> Faint as shed flowers, the attenuated dream.[1]

'The Stream's Secret' anticipates this 'hour', when

> . . . I and she
> Slake in one kiss the thirst of memory.

In his much-favoured spatial imagery, Rossetti writes of
'Heart's anguish in the impenetrable maze' and of arriving
at last at a state of perfect communion in love:

> And as in the dim grove,
> When the rains cease that hushed them long,
> 'Mid glistening boughs the song-birds wake to song, –
> So from our hearts deep-shrined in love,
> While the leaves throb, beneath, around, above,
> The quivering notes shall throng.

The past threatens this communion, as in 'Willowwood',
and the familiar animating imagery functions effectively:

> . . . Nay, why
> Name the dead hours? I mind them well:

[1] The image of the last line recalls the dropped rose leaves of 'Willowwood'
(iv).

> Their ghosts in many darkened doorways dwell
> With desolate eyes to know them by.

'Love's hour' when the lovers will meet is, like the hour of 'Stillborn Love', biding the time of its coming but, though its arrival is anticipated with joy, the long wait through separation and frustration is imagined more vividly:

> Its soul remembers yet
> Those sunless hours that passed it by;
> And still it hears the night's disconsolate cry,
> And feels the branches wringing wet
> Cast on its brow, that may not once forget,
> Dumb tears from the blind sky.

Rossetti's choice of a stream as the dominant image of his poem precedes William James's likening of our fluid and continuously changing human consciousness to a river. His phrase, 'the stream of thought, of consciousness, or of subjective life', has been accepted ever since. Rossetti's stream is an image of more than one value. Like James's, it is a flow of consciousness which bears with it other images from the depth of the psyche. It is also a reflecting medium and so an image of introspection – this is especially important in the first 'Willowwood' sonnet where the poet and Love bend together over the water. In addition, it is an image of time, the ever-rolling stream which bears all its sons away. Rossetti admired Tennyson's poem, 'The Brook',[1] and was not likely to leave unnoted the refrain:

> For men may come and men may go,
> But I go on for ever.

Sonnet LXXXIV of *The House of Life* ('Farewell to the Glen', 1869–70) associates a stream with the same idea:

> Sweet stream-fed glen, why say 'farewell' to thee
> Who far'st so well and find'st for ever smooth
> The brow of Time where men may read no ruth?

[1] *Letters*, i, p. 267.

In 'The Stream's Secret' the waters lead, as does the course of a lifetime, to death. Love, Life and Death, Rossetti's trinity, group themselves at the end of the poem and in the waters of death, as in the waters of Lethe, the past will at last be laid to rest. The penultimate stanza claims that love will triumph beyond death but the final images are of cold and grief.

'The Stream's Secret' is more discursive, more explicit than the Willowwood sonnets. It does not achieve the same degree of intense concentration. The mood is ambiguous, alternating between hope and a sense that hope is illusory, but the effect of the sharply focused scene in the sonnets is beyond its range. The kiss which the lover in 'The Stream's Secret' expects to slake the thirst of memory, though the 'dead hours' stand round about, in 'Willowwood' does no such thing. The diffused effects of the longer poem achieve a definition in the sonnets which is in fact far more suggestive.

Because the Willowwood sonnets are so remarkable, 'The Stream's Secret' has in comparison to be described as weaker but in itself it is by no means a negligible poem. The six-line stanza with its clever patterning of interlaced couplets and quatrains and its fluctuating line lengths creates the ripple of waters as they meet and withdraw: 'While the whispering music of the water is suggested by onomatopoeic sound repetition, its wandering flow is represented by the wavering movement, as opposed to a steady rhythm, produced by the stanza arrangement of intermixed trimeter, tetrameter and pentameter lines; no lines of equal length occur consecutively.'[1] The metrical skill enhances the effect of the imagery which takes us, at its best moments, into a surreal landscape of inner experience, only describable in terms of 'an unspeakably mysterious bond' between 'outward and inward matters':

[1] Joseph F. Vogel, *Dante Gabriel Rossetti's Versecraft* (University of Florida Humanities Monograph, no. 34, 1971, p. 51).

> How should all this be told? –
> All the sad sum of wayworn days; –
> Heart's anguish in the impenetrable maze;
> And on the waste uncoloured wold
> The visible burden of the sun grown cold
> And the moon's labouring gaze?

The water imagery used in poems just discussed is related to consciousness, introspection and time but water appears in many contexts in Rossetti's imagery and is a symbol almost as intimate as that of the birds and leafy grove. The two are associated in 'A Last Confession' when the dying man describes the girl as she was when he first loved her:

> . . . Her great eyes,
> That sometimes turned half dizzily beneath
> The passionate lids, as faint, when she would speak,
> Had also in them hidden springs of mirth,
> Which under the dark lashes evermore
> Shook to her laugh, as when a bird flies low
> Between the water and the willow-leaves,
> And the shade quivers till he wins the light.

The same tissue of images recurs a little later again, to express the man's passionate love:

> Then silent to the soul I held my way:
> And from the fountains of the public place
> Unto the pigeon-haunted pinnacles,
> Bright wings and water winnowed the bright air;
> And stately with her laugh's subsiding smile
> She went . . .

Standing water makes a powerful image of the sub-conscious in 'The Bride's Prelude':

> Her thought, long stagnant, stirred by speech,
> Gave her a sick recoil;
> As, dip thy fingers through the green
> That masks a pool – where they have been
> The naked depth is black between.

And the sea, whether 'iron-bosomed' like time itself or an unnamed threat, sounds frequently through the poems as when, in 'Love's Nocturn', the poet descends to the 'sunken beach' where the shades of men are found:

> Groping in the windy stair,
> (Darkness and the breath of space
> Like loud waters everywhere).

Rossetti's imagery of the outer and inner world is the product of personal insight and real poetic originality. He himself realised that its nature would not be easily recognised and he tried at times to write more popularly. The poem 'Down Stream', written at Kelmscott in 1871 – at about the same time, that is, as 'Willowwood', 'The Stream's Secret' and poems associated with them – is an example: 'rather out of my usual way', Rossetti wrote, 'rude aiming at the sort of popular view that Tennyson perhaps alone succeeds in taking'.[1] The scene is again a stream or river and the topic is the griefs of love but the material which the poem shares with 'Willowwood' and 'The Stream's Secret' is translated into more conventional terms. Lovers part in 'Down Stream' but the situation is the old familiar story of seduction, desertion and suicide. The contrast between the tragedies of human experience and the indifferent face of nature is clearly made, as the river in which the girl and her child have drowned presents a calm and fresh face to a new generation of schoolchildren in a new summer. The flow of the river parallels the flow of time as the months are marked off in each stanza of the poem. But the river is not here a stream of consciousness and the natural description is limited to mirroring the stages of the story, reflecting in turn kindness and laughter, parting and tears, storm and desperation. Tennyson, Rossetti remarks in the letter quoted, 'tries to get within hail of general readers. But I fear, however much I might like to do so, that it's not my vocation except in such a trifle as this once in a way; and I dare say', he adds glumly, 'this would be

[1] *Letters*, iii, p. 958.

voted obscure.' When he sent a revised version of 'Down Stream' to his mother a week or two later, he apologetically explained the function of the natural description.[1]

In the psychological area which he cultivated, introspection of a small but intimate and sensitive region of the psyche, Rossetti was an explorer ahead of his time. The imagery which he evolved to express his findings and the way he handled it were also out of period. He had not enough confidence to go his own way and trust to time to justify him but too often diluted his own vision to make his writing more like other people's and more acceptable, he hoped, to contemporaries. The penalty has been that later generations who might have acclaimed him as a remarkable symbolist poet have written him down as a practitioner of minor Victorian modes. The area over which Rossetti's imagination works most effectively is small and, because of this and because of the intensity of the energies released, it seems inevitable that the best writing should occur only in short passages or poems. Attempts at greater length are almost always a failure and, as in 'The Stream's Secret' for example, the effect of individually potent images is weakened by surroundings in which the imaginative pressure is low. There are some exceptional occasions on which Rossetti succeeds, at any rate to a considerable extent, in sustaining a longer poem but these occur when he is dealing with subjects other than that inner exploration which is his special forte. Then other gifts are brought into play, in 'The Burden of Nineveh', for example, a satiric wit, and in 'Jenny', a dramatic instinct for character and situation. These are very accomplished poems. Even so, they are too long and the most memorable parts of them are images evoked by themes which stimulate Rossetti's strongest responses – the shadow which remains when time has removed generations of men in 'The Burden of Nineveh' and Lust as 'a toad within a stone' in 'Jenny',

[1] Ibid., p. 976.

living on though all else crumbles, an inalienable presence so long as man endures. The brevity and concentration of the sonnet make it the perfect form for Rossetti and its independence of narrative or discourse makes the sonnet sequence the ideal structure.

The psychological basis of Rossetti's imagery has implications also for his language, a feature of his work which has often been thought to be specially vulnerable. There is probably not much room for fruitful comment on the usages which are part and parcel of the medieval subjects which Rossetti often chose. A reader whose taste rejects nineteenth-century medievalism and another who finds a charm in it will estimate the archaisms differently. It is fair to point out, however, that the pervasiveness of Rossetti's medievalism is sometimes exaggerated. He can and does employ a good contemporary language when he chooses. In 'A Last Confession', the blank verse accommodates the knocking in of a nail on which to hang a glass ornament, much better than Tennyson's adapts itself to buying and selling in the little shop in 'Enoch Arden'. Similarly no affected diction is required or used in 'Jenny' to state what Saturday night in the Haymarket means to the girls who walk the streets. The most interesting aspect of Rossetti's language in the present context, however, is the style he developed for sonnets written in the late 1860s and the 1870s. It is a strongly marked style and its emphases and idiosyncrasies may well be found objectionable unless they can be shown to be justified. At this point, recognition of the basis of the predominant imagery becomes a very relevant factor, for the heavily charged language is evolved, as is the imagery, to communicate what Rossetti sees when he shuts himself in with his soul. He fashions a language, as he fashions a vocabulary of images, to serve this end.

The characteristics of the late sonnet style include unfamiliar words – 'refluent', for example, and 'philtred euphracy' – and words used with uncommon etymological exactness: 'inveteracy of ill' (xciii), 'vanished hours and hours eventual' (xxxvi). Compound epithets and nouns, often original coinings, abound:

> Thine eyes grey-lit in shadowing hair above (viii)

> Because our talk was of the cloud-control
> And moon-track of the journeying face of Fate (xlv)

Some lines carry a heavy burden of polysyllables and the whole highly wrought complex is illustrated in sonnet xli, 'Through Death to Love'. The first few lines of the sonnet will serve as specimen:

> Like labour-laden moonclouds faint to flee
> From winds that sweep the winter-bitten wold –
> Like multiform circumfluence manifold
> Of night's flood-tide – like terrors that agree
> Of hoarse-tongued fire and inarticulate sea.[1]

On this and passages like it some words of Pater's offer a helpful commentary. For Rossetti, he wrote, 'life is a crisis at every moment. A sustained impressibility towards the mysterious conditions of man's everyday life, towards the very mystery itself in it, gives a singular gravity to all his work.'[2] This reflects the mood of the late sonnets well and points to the conclusion that though the language in which Rossetti expresses himself may well seem overcharged by ordinary standards, ordinary standards do not apply. Sonnet no. xli, whose opening has been quoted above, has as its theme the apparent conflict between Death and Love and the octave evokes the terror of death. The imagery of wind and sea is couched in strongly stressed, alliterative language charged with emotional suggestion. The 'multiform circumfluence manifold/Of night's flood-tide' creates by its long heavy words and repeated sounds a sense of a clinging, stifling, indefeasible presence encroaching

---

[1] Vogel, *Rossetti's Versecraft* has an interesting discussion of Rossetti's vocabulary on pp. 12–19.
[2] Pater, *Appreciations*, p. 220.

inexorably on an unprotected life. As a description of darkness the phrasing is merely mannered but as a concentrated expression of the horrors of death experienced in night-time's terror, it generates some power. The description of desolation and fear in the opening lines is balanced by the equally intense and verbally elaborate picture of hope in the final tercet:

> Tell me, my heart – what angel-greeted door
> Or threshold of wing-winnowed threshing-floor
> Hath guest fire-fledged as thine, whose Lord is Love?

These extreme statements of polarities record intense psychological pressures and the language itself is under pressure to demonstrate strong reaction rather than merely to describe it.

Sonnet no. XLVI is also a night poem:

> What shall be said of this embattled day
> And armèd occupation of this night
> By all thy foes beleagured – now when sight
> Nor sound denotes the loved one far away?
> Of these thy vanquished hours what shalt thou say –
> As every sense to which she dealt delight
> Now labours lonely o'er the stark noon-height
> To reach the sunset's desolate disarray?
>
> Stand still, fond fettered wretch! while Memory's art
> Parades the Past before thy face, and lures
> Thy spirit to her passionate portraitures:
> Till the tempestuous tide-gates flung apart
> Flood with wild will the hollows of thy heart
> And thy heart rends thee, and thy body endures.

This is a better poem than no. XLI, sustained by dramatic movement throughout, but the two poems share the same characteristics of extravagant image and highly-wrought language. When in a later day D. H. Lawrence gave words to the inner consciousness of his characters he similarly spoke of earthquakes where the eye of common-sense might acknowledge no more than a tremor. When Hermione Roddice enters the church for

the Crich wedding, and fails to see Birkin standing beside
the altar as she expected: 'A terrible storm came over her,
as if she were drowning. She was possessed by a devas-
tating helplessness . . . Never had she known such a pang
of utter and final hopelessness. It was beyond death, so
utterly null, desert.'[1] Lawrence's language, and that of
Rossetti in later sonnets, is in a different register from
ordinary usage. Its referents have to be sought among
the shocks and spasms which occur out of sight and
unmanifested except, perhaps, by a momentary expression
or gesture. Rossetti's inward gaze is always intense and
what he sees is a drama so vivid and compelling that he
must couch it in language which challenges attention by
its own intensity and selfconsciousness:

> Some prisoned moon in steep cloud-fastnesses –
> Throned queen and thralled; some dying sun whose pyre
> Blazed with momentous memorable fire; –
> Who hath not yearned and fed his heart with these?
> Who, sleepless, hath not anguished to appease
> Tragical shadow's realm of sound and sight
> Conjectured in the lamentable night? . . .
> Lo! the soul's sphere of infinite images!
>
> What sense shall count them? Whether it forecast
> The rose-winged hours that flutter in the van
> Of Love's unquestioning unrevealed span –
> Visions of golden futures: or that last
> Wild pageant of the accumulated past
> That clangs and flashes for a drowning man.
>
>   (no. LXII, 'The Soul's Sphere')

    The language of these sonnets is a remarkable creation,
capable of striking successes after its rarefied fashion but
subject to failures all the more blatant because of the
sonority of the writing. Sonnet no. XXXIV, 'The Dark
Glass', is a case in point with its muddled images in the
octave and weak final tercet. Yet the first line of this
sonnet, 'Not I myself know all my love for thee', is a

---

[1] *Women in Love*, chapter 1.

dramatic one and the whole poem, if it is not among Rossetti's successes, does bring sharply to attention the importance of a subject which is at the root of nearly all Rossetti's work, his view of love. Rossetti's most probing psychological explorations are motivated by his fascination with the mystery of love and consideration of what this meant to him will lead to a further view of that sensitive spot, the leafy grove to which so much of the imagery takes us. Sometimes it is the 'rustling covert' of his soul, where the bird of love wings joyful way, sometimes a 'devious' covert of 'dismay' and sometimes a place of 'polluted coverts' where 'changing footpaths shift and fall' and 'Miserable phantoms sigh' ('Love's Nocturn'). In his religion of love Rossetti is both priest and infidel: here is the most radical of the splits in his nature and it conditions everything else. In tracing the fissure we shall find ourselves returning to the young man who sketched Dante drawing an angel and also to Rossetti, the man of his own time, who shared the ideas and interests of mid-nineteenth-century society.

4

'Venus Verticordia'

'MAY one be a devil and not know it?' The question is
asked by the painter Chiaro dell'Erma in Rossetti's early
story, *Hand and Soul*. He has painted allegorical pictures
of Peace, determined to 'put his hand to no other works
but only to such as had for their end the presentment of
some moral greatness that should influence the beholder',[1]
but, on a day of religious festival, a feud between rival
families in Pisa breaks out in violence 'and there was so
much blood cast up the walls on a sudden, that it ran in
long streams down Chiaro's paintings'.[2] Chiaro, seeing
this, asks his question. He has striven to lead men to
righteousness but they have not followed and, worse
than this, perhaps he has even alienated them from the
truth by the imperfection of his treatment of it. If so,
unconsciously but effectively, he has done the devil's
work.

The crisis is resolved by his vision of the woman who
is his soul. His work as an artist is not to be fulfilled in
the quest for fame, she tells him, nor by endeavouring to
become a moral teacher. Instead he must seek to know
himself and to be true to himself. On her instruction, he
paints her portrait so that the image of his soul will be
always before him and, as he paints, his doubts and per-
plexities fall away and he finds rest. The vision of the
soul and her admonitions are presented as authoritative
and decisive but the religious language and mystical
trappings scarcely conceal the fact that the message is
thin and its application doubtful. We are told that as

[1] *Works*, i, p. 388.
[2] Ibid., p. 390.

Chiaro worked on the portrait 'his face grew solemn with knowledge'[1] but what he learned is not specified and indeed, the very young Rossetti could hardly be expected to know. As he grew older he knew better, and then he had a different story to tell.

To look into his soul and discern the scenes and movements in the recesses of consciousness was the task to which Rossetti's temperament and imagination led him. What he saw in his maturity reflects far more the painful uncertainty of Chiaro before the vision appears than the serene purity of the vision itself. The lesson that experience taught him was that God's work and the devil's, vice and virtue, purity and corruption, lie close to each other and the one can always be confounded in the other. A slight shift of position, and what has been taken as an emblem of salvation becomes a mark of damnation. This is the central moral insight of Rossetti's work, one of which he was fully aware but which he regretted. In July 1858 he wrote, more sadly than playfully, to Charles Eliot Norton, congratulating him on the name of the Massachusetts estate where he lived:

Your 'Shady Hill' is a tempting address, where one would wish to be. It reminds one somehow of the *Pilgrim's Progress* where the pleasant names of Heavenly places really make you feel as if you could get there if the journey could only be made in that very way – the pitfalls plain to the eye and all the wicked people with wicked names.[2]

Twelve years later, writing to the same correspondent, he expressed more paradoxically his awareness that vice and virtue are not easily disentangled. The idea gives a sombre tone to an apology for delay in answering a letter: 'I am truly ashamed of the above date, and all my sins of omission; including perhaps some omitted sins – for these too strike one as mistakes occasionally as life wears on.'[3]

[1] Ibid., p. 395.
[2] *Letters*, i, p. 340.
[3] *Letters*, ii, p. 783.

In the previous year (1869) he had written one of his grimmest sonnets, 'Vain Virtues' (no. LXXXV):

> What is the sorriest thing that enters Hell?
> None of the sins – but this and that fair deed
> Which a soul's sin at length could supersede.
> These yet are virgins, whom death's timely knell
> Might once have sainted; whom the fiends compel
> Together now, in snake-bound shuddering sheaves
> Of anguish, while the pit's pollution leaves
> Their refuse maidenhood abominable.
>
> Night sucks them down, the tribute of the pit,
> Whose names, half entered in the book of Life,
> Were God's desire at noon. And as their hair
> And eyes sink last, the Torturer deigns no whit
> To gaze, but, yearning, waits his destined wife,
> The Sin still blithe on earth that sent them there.

Though the imagery of this sonnet can have more than one application, the most obvious reference is sexual. Love polluted and become lust or hatred, the worship of beauty become sensual idolatry: paraphrased in such terms, the sonnet points to the Janus face of Love and Beauty as it appears in so many of Rossetti's poems. 'Vain Virtues' gives a reverse image of 'The Blessed Damozel'. There the love of the man and woman was a blessed quality and the Damozel, in heaven, could seek redemption for her lover on earth because he loved her and she him. She was a *donna angelicata* in a heaven of lovers, acting upon him for his salvation, to lead him upwards. The sonnet is a grim duplication of the earlier poem, from the perspective of hell. In the sonnet, souls are sucked down, not mounting up, and the demon in hell, hideous counterpart of the blessed damozel, yearns and waits for his destined wife who, on earth, gleefully prepares souls for perdition. 'Vain Virtues' faces, without palliatives, the horror of the possibility that the pursuit of love may lead to the devil after all. Fair deeds are distorted into vileness, the blessed damozel is turned into a destroyer of souls, the yearning of lovers parted by death is gruesomely parodied in hell: these are not isolated transformations in the world of Rossetti's poetry but have their analogues everywhere.

'What more inspiring for poetic effort', Rossetti wrote in his answer to Buchanan, 'than the terrible Love turned to Hate – perhaps the deadliest of all passion-woven complexities – which is the theme of "Sister Helen", and, in a more fantastic form, of "Eden Bower" – the surroundings of both poems being the mere machinery of a central universal meaning?'[1] Buchanan had caught a glimpse of the cloven hoof in Rossetti's poetry but not understood the tension which it portended. Rossetti does not care to rewrite in prose what Buchanan had failed to understand in verse but the phrase 'passion-woven complexities' is, in fact, a revealing one and 'Sister Helen' is a specially good illustration of it. The poem was first published in 1853 but Rossetti worked over it again in 1870 and 1881 making a small but significant change in 1870 which added yet another strand to the weave of complex passions which the poem treats. The story is one of sexual love variously perverted and become destructive. Keith of Ewerne was unfaithful. Sister Helen is motivated in her vengeance by embittered, thwarted passion. Another counter-image of the blessed damozel, she is driving her lover to hell instead of drawing him to heaven and, as she melts his wax-effigy before the fire, she prefigures the devils of the infernal pit tormenting the souls of the damned in flame. This is a vision of love as damnation and though there is other love in the poem too, the father's love for his son in agony and the bride's love for her guilty husband, both father and bride suffer because of the corrupt passions of Keith of Ewerne and Sister Helen. In 1870 Rossetti complicated the emotional situation by allowing Sister Helen, even while implacably pursuing her vengeance, to retain some sense of the former sympathy which

[1] *Works*, i, p. 486.

existed between her and Keith of Ewerne. The ante-
penultimate stanza originally read:

> 'Oh the wind is sad in the iron chill,
>   Sister Helen,
> And weary sad they look by the hill.'
> 'But Keith of Ewerne's sadder still,
>   Little brother'

Rossetti changed Sister Helen's response so that the final
version reads:

> But he and I are sadder still

and he pointed out to Hall Caine that this line and the
last spoken by Sister Helen – 'A soul that's lost as mine
is lost, Little brother' – show that she and her victim
share a 'mutual misery'.[1] Through all chimes the repeated
refrain, 'O Mother, Mary Mother', the invocation of the
Virgin being the final element in this most fraught of
'passion-woven complexities'. The blessed damozel
planned also to appeal to 'the lady Mary', confident of
her sympathy with lovers, but divine and human love are
extensions of each other in that poem whereas in 'Sister
Helen' they are pitifully at odds.

A later composed ballad, 'The King's Tragedy', makes
another variant on the love–hate theme. The love of the
poet-king, James I of Scotland, and his queen, is deep
and tender and contrasted with the black hatred of Sir
Robert Graeme. But after the king's death, the queen
becomes a figure of implacable vengeance, all her being
concentrated in hatred on his murderers. Kate Barlass
reports to her as they are captured:

> And still as I told her day by day,
> Her pallor changed to sight,
> And the frost grew to a furnace-flame
> That burnt her visage white.

---

[1] T. Hall Caine, *Recollections of Dante Gabriel Rossetti* (London, 1882), p.
129.

When, after 'torments fierce and dire', all are dead, she kisses the dead king:

> And whispered low with a strange proud smile –
> 'James, James, they suffered more!'

Loving as she is and the object of the King's devotion, Queen Jane is surprisingly akin to Sister Helen. The passion of love in both engenders a grim and unrelenting cruelty, though 'Sister Helen' is the more purely dramatic and effective poem.

'Then I saw that there was a way to hell, even from the gates of heaven', Bunyan wrote, and though Rossetti may have read *Pilgrim's Progress* at too early an age to recognise a truth so near the quick of his own experience, his theology of love and beauty was not long in achieving the same perception. 'Jenny', begun in 1848 but composed mainly in 1858–9, and 'A Last Confession', belonging to approximately the same periods, give striking expression to his perennial awareness of the shiftiness of ideals, whereby love and beauty become lust and squalor by easy but irreversible transition. The melting of one image into another constitutes crucial moments in both poems. As the young man of 'Jenny' looks at Jenny's beauty and thinks of her past, present and future, 'The woman almost fades from view' and he sees instead

> A cipher of man's changeless sum
> Of lust, past, present and to come.

So also, in 'A Last Confession', the laugh of the girl whom the patriot loves turns into the laugh of the 'brown-shouldered harlot' who sells her favours to the Austrians. Love again takes on the aspect of hate and he murders what he adores and is thenceforward haunted by remorse, unresolved suspicion and unsatisfied longing till he dies. Images of heaven and hell abound in 'A Last Confession':

> . . . How should I show
> The heart that glowed then with love's heat, each day
> More and more brightly? . . .

the man asks, as he remembers how:

> . . . for long years now
> The very flame that flew about the heart,
> And gave it fiery wings, has come to be
> The lapping blaze of hell's environment
> Whose tongues all bid the molten heart despair.

In a powerful passage Heaven and Hell change into each other, just as the girl's laugh and the harlot's also become one. The man tries to convey to the father-confessor what it was like to realise that his love for her was not returned. 'What do you love?' he asks. 'Your Heaven?'

> . . . Conceive it spread
> For one first year of all eternity
> All round you with all joys and gifts of God;
> And then when most your soul is blest with it
> And all yields song together – then it stands
> O'the sudden like a pool that once gave back
> Your image, but now drowns it and is clear
> Again – or like a sun bewitched that burns
> Your shadow from you, and still shines in sight.
> How could you bear it? Would you not cry out,
> Among those eyes grown blind to you, those ears
> That hear no more your voice you hear the same –
> 'God! what is left but hell for company,
> But hell, hell, hell?' – until the name so breathed
> Whirled with hot wind and sucked you down in fire?

In both 'A Last Confession' and 'Jenny', such images of horrid transformation are reinforced by descriptions which function ironically. The child whom the partisan finds on the Italian hillside:

> . . . might have served a painter to portray
> That heavenly child which in the latter days
> Shall walk between the lion and the lamb.

In the other poem the young man reflects on Jenny also as a painter's model:

> Fair shines the golden aureole
> In which our highest painters place
> Some living woman's simple face.

And the stilled features thus descried
As Jenny's long throat droops aside –
The shadows where the cheeks are thin,
And pure wide curve from ear to chin –
With Raffael's, Leonardo's hand
To show them to men's souls, might stand,
Whole ages long, the whole world through,
For preachings of what God can do.

The pairing of opposites to indicate the deep bonds of kinship between them is one of the earliest structural ideas of 'Jenny'. In an early version in the Fitzwilliam Museum, Cambridge, the lines 'Hath not the potter power over the clay, of the same lump to make one vessel unto honour and another unto dishonour?' (Romans, ix. 21), form the epigraph, and the passage about 'Cousin Nell', which a modern reader may be tempted to think dispensable, is in fact a vital part of the original conception. She and Jenny are two faces of beautiful, young girlhood:

> . . . for honour and dishonour made,
> Two sister vessels . . .

The idea is conventional enough until, typically for Rossetti, the outlines of each begin to unsettle and one merges into the other:

So pure – so fall'n! How dare to think
Of the first common, kindred link?
Yet, Jenny, till the world shall burn
It seems that all things take their turn;
And who shall say but this fair tree
May need, in changes that may be,
Your children's children's charity?
Scorned then, no doubt, as you are scorn'd!
Shall no man hold his pride forewarn'd
Till in the end, the Day of Days,
At Judgement, one of his own race,
As frail and lost as you, shall rise –
His daughter, with his mother's eyes?

Time, which always stimulates Rossetti's imagination, is the agent of change here and the passage makes the same deliberate disturbance of view-point and produces the same shocked recognition of the work of years as is to be found in the sonnet 'Inclusiveness'.

Time plays its part also in the brilliant and compassionate lines on the prostitute's career:

> Our learned London children know,
> Poor Jenny, all your pride and woe;
> Have seen your lifted silken skirt
> Advertise dainties through the dirt;
> Have seen your coach-wheels splash rebuke
> On virtue; and have learned your look
> When, wealth and health slipped past, you stare
> Along the streets alone, and there,
> Round the long park, across the bridge,
> The cold lamps at the pavement's edge
> Wind on together and apart,
> A fiery serpent for your heart.[1]

But this, though so finely imagined, is a matter of simple sequentiality. More distinctive in Rossetti is his trick of imposing one picture upon another, whether it be the overlaying of an image drawn from one generation upon that of another or whether it be the appearance of a devilish grimace upon the face of an angel. On occasions the two possibilities are combined.[2]

Rossetti's awareness of the instability of virtue and

---

[1] The image of the last four lines is pictorialised in the painting 'Found'.

[2] In a manuscript volume in the Fitzwilliam Museum, Cambridge, occur these lines, entitled 'One Girl (Adaptation from Sappho)':

I

Like the sweet apple which reddens upon the topmost bough,
Atop on the topmost twig – which the pluckers forgot somehow –
Forgot it not, nay, but got it not, for none could get it till now.

II

Like the wild hyacinth flower which on the hills is found,
Which the passing feet of the shepherds for ever tear and wound,
Until the purple blossom is trodden into the ground.

These triplets are a striking rendering of the double image which is at the heart of 'Jenny' and many other poems. They are printed in the 1911 edition of *Works*, edited by W. M. Rossetti, under the title 'Beauty. A Combination from Sappho'.

vice expresses itself in superimposed images whose referents need not be restricted to the areas of experience which he himself most cultivated. The ambivalence of love and beauty as objects of pursuit receives more explicit but at the same time more limited treatment in a number of works which have a dominant motif in common. This consists of the opposition between a siren and a pure love and one of its most extensive and effective appearances is in the prose tale *The Orchard Pit*. This story was written in 1869, twenty years after *Hand and Soul* and *Saint Agnes of Intercession*, and it leaves no doubt that the confident, if somewhat vague, morality of Chiaro dell'Erma has been clouded over with more disturbing knowledge. The mystery of previous existence which begins to open upon the young painter in the second story has also taken a darker colour and the sense of inescapable destiny lies heavy over the first person narrator of *The Orchard Pit*. The story begins: 'Men tell me that sleep has many dreams; but all my life I have dreamt one dream alone.'[1] This obsessive dream is of a glen, the slopes of which are covered with wild apple-trees. In the largest of them stands a golden-haired and beautiful woman who sings and holds out a red apple as if offering it to someone coming down the slope. Beneath her, there is only a tangle of trees, stretching across the dried-up bed of a stream, but in the pit at the bottom of the glen lie the bodies of men who, from olden times to the present, have eaten her apples and died with the bitten fruit in their hands. The glen is well-known to the narrator, not in dreams only but also in his waking life. He knows that one day he will see the Siren there and that he will die in that place. This consummation to come, the fate that he is driven towards, seems to him the only reality in his life and the pleasures and duties of his existence among men seem to be a dream.

The narrator is engaged to be married to a woman who

[1] *Works*, i. p. 427.

loves him dearly and one day she offers him an apple
from the Siren's dell and makes him sit with her beneath
the Siren's tree. She stands in the branches like the fatal
woman and holds out an apple but when she tries to sing,
she cannot: 'at that moment she cried out, and leaped
from the tree into my arms, and said that the leaves were
whispering other words to her, and my name among
them'.[1] When she throws the apple away among the
tangled boughs at the bottom of the dell, a little snake
appears. Finally the 'I' of the story dreams his dream,
perhaps for the last time, and enacts in it his own end. In
the dream he goes to the dell with his love. The moon
shines full in the sky like the sun at mid-day and, though
it is autumn, the apple-trees bear both fruit and blossom
together. He sees the Siren's hand holding an apple out
to him and he hears her song. His betrothed tries to hold
him back but he fights his way down the slope, scattering
other fruit in his rough progress, for he will take only the
one apple from the Siren's hand. The branches, as he
pushes his way through them, spring back and tear the
hands and face of his beloved. 'Come to Love', the Siren
sings, and next, 'Come to Life', and both Love and Life
seem sweet as she sings of them. Then at last she says
'Come to Death', 'and Death's name in her mouth was
the very swoon of all sweetest things that be'. She kisses
him once as he takes the apple, he bites into it and falls
crashing into the pit among the dead white faces awaiting
him. After this dream, the narrator awakes but he feels
that his end is near.

The symbolism of this needs no commentary but the
role of the young man's betrothed is worth noticing. She
senses a threat to her hold over her lover and when she
offers him the apple and tries to sing the Siren's song to
him, it is in an effort to rival the sensuous appeal of the
Siren – a hopeless one, just as her attempt to keep him
back in his last dash down the slope will be hopeless. In

[1] Ibid., p. 429.

the five stanzas which are all that Rossetti wrote of a
verse version of the story, he retains the image which he
used in the prose to describe the relation between the
man and the girl as the man sees it:

> My Love I call her, and she loves me well:
> But I love her as in the maelstrom cup
> The whirled stone loves the leaf inseparable
> That clings to it round all the circling swell,
> And that the same last eddy swallows up.

The image states clearly that the Siren destroys the innocent girl as well as the lover, though in the man's dream
of his end he speaks of last seeing her 'lifting... her hands
to heaven as she cried aloud above me, while I still
forced my way downwards'.[1] Her fate is prefigured in the
prose tale by that of the sweetheart of the young man's
brother. He had already, we are told, succumbed to the
Siren's lure and she, in going to seek him, had met her
own death. The inexorable passion of the men blasts them
all. Corrupted and innocent alike are destroyed by the
Siren's spell.

The words of the Siren's song are also to be noted.
First she sang 'Come to Love', then ' "Come to Life"...
But long before I reached her, she knew that all her will
was mine: and then her voice rose softer than ever, and
her words were, "Come to Death".' In 1869, the year of
writing *The Orchard Pit*, Rossetti published sixteen
sonnets which were later to be part of *The House of Life*
sequence and he entitled them 'Of Life, Love and Death'.
The Orchard Pit alerts us to the fact that in Rossetti's
usage these words are full of questions. The Siren
promises love and through love the sweets of life but she
is in reality a figure of death. The narrator who tells his
dream will join the others who have been her victims and
who seem, as they lie in the pit, to be aware of their own
state – 'I felt my crashing fall through the tangled boughs

[1] Ibid., p. 430.

beneath her feet, and saw the dead white faces that wel-
comed me in the pit.'[1]

The Doom of the Sirens is a sketch for a lyrical tragedy
and basically it comprises variations on the theme of *The
Orchard Pit*. Again an innocent love, this time his bride,
contends with a siren for the hero. This time he resists
the Siren's lure and the fatal spell which she casts over
men is broken, but, so dire is the struggle, that despite
his victory the man dies. As Rossetti puts it: 'he...
though proof against her lures and loathing her in his
heart, is physically absorbed into the death-agony of the
expiring spell'.[2] His bride, meanwhile, is praying for him
but as he dies he calls to her and she answers his call by
joining him in death. The implication seems to be that
they will be reunited in some other world, having both
earned a lovers' heaven, but Rossetti never attempted to
develop more fully this story of the fall of the Siren and
the moral triumph of the protagonist. In contrast, the
appearances of the fatal woman with all her power un-
impaired are many and various in his poetry. She is
Lilith in 'Eden Bower' and in *The House of Life* sonnet,
'Body's Beauty' (no. LXXVIII, 1867). She is Helen in 'Troy
Town' and in the two 'Cassandra' sonnets. She is Circe
in the sonnet 'The Wine of Circe' which gives a keen
dramatic sense of what it is to be caught in her spell. The
destined victims present themselves:

> Lords of their hour, they come. And by her knee
> Those cowering beasts, their equals heretofore
> Wait; who with them in new equality
> To-night shall echo back the sea's dull roar
> With a vain wail from passion's tide-strown shore
> Where the dishevelled sea-weed hates the sea.

The symbols of the sonnet 'Venus Verticordia' link the
Siren of *The Orchard Pit* and Helen of Troy. Here the
Siren hesitates, the apple in her hand. The flames of Troy

[1] Ibid.
[2] Ibid., p. 436.

symbolise the ruin that will come if she gives it. The sonnet was written for a picture and William Rossetti reported to his brother the result of some research in Lemprière's classical dictionary: 'Lemprière makes a very startling statement', he writes, and goes on to quote it: 'Venus was also surnamed Verticordia, because she could turn the hearts of women to cultivate chastity', and he adds: 'just the contrary sort of Venus from the one you contemplate'.[1] On this warning from his brother, Rossetti cut out 'Verticordia' from the title but he restored it in 1881, suitably enough since the ambiguity of Venus's role which it suggests is a subject which dominates much of his writing.

The siren-pure love nexus as it appears in these and other examples can be described as simply a matter of a highly-sexed Rossetti hag-ridden by Victorian prudery and no doubt such an account represents at least part of the truth. What is interesting, however, in situations like this is not the factor which poets have in common with other men, but those qualities in their minds and imaginations which turn shared property into something individual and rare. To arrive at understanding of these qualities in Rossetti we have to pursue two paths but we find that they ultimately converge in one.

To begin with, there are his attempts at reconciling body and soul in what is envisaged as an ideal love relationship. That daring poem 'The Blessed Damozel' challenges the reader to notice the warmth of the girl's bosom and claims implicitly that sex may become sacred. Soul and soul penetrate in the heaven of 'The Portrait' and in this consummation find God. In a letter of August 1869 Rossetti commented on the last line of his sonnet 'For a Venetian Pastoral by Giorgione': 'It gives. . . the momentary contact with the immortal which results from sensuous culmination and is always a half-conscious

---

[1] Quoted in *Letters*, ii, p. 727, note 3. The date is given as August 1859 but this is evidently a mistake for 1869.

element of it.'[1] The sonnet itself is one of his most remarkable performances, so sensuous that it is itself almost equivalent to a physical caress, but the heat, the silence, the lapsed activity, the gaze whose direction cannot be determined, all suggest the presence of a mystery, an experience arrived at through physical climax but not completed by it.

There are more conventional attempts to justify the demands of the body. Sonnet no. ix of *The House of Life* (1869), called 'Passion and Worship', is one. The sestet includes a typical Rossettian interior landscape but for once it fails to generate any imaginative life. The lyric, 'Love-Lily', originally intended for inclusion in *The House of Life*, has much in common with 'Passion and Worship' but is more interesting. In both poems two aspects of love are personified, flame-winged Passion and white-winged Worship in one and, in the other, a spirit born of the physical attributes of the beloved:

> . . . whose birth endows
> My blood with fire to burn through me

and a second spirit brought to birth in her heart and soul:

> . . . who lifts apart
> His tremulous wings and looks at me;
> Who on my mouth his finger lays,
> And shows, while whispering lutes confer,
> That Eden of Love's watered ways
> Whose winds and spirits worship her.

The interior landscape is here made more graceful than in the sonnet by the music of the verse form. The final stanza produces first a plea that the poet may be able to etherealise desire and share the purity of the girl but then, like Sir Philip Sidney's Astrophil when bound to chastity by Stella, he cries in recoil for physical fulfilment after all. Rossetti's poem concludes with lines that lead to the furthest point of his vision of reconciliation between passion and pure love:

[1] *Letters*, ii, p. 727.

> Ah! let not hope be still distraught,
> But find in her its gracious goal,
> Whose speech Truth knows not from her thought
> Nor Love her body from her soul.

The last line is echoed in sonnet v of *The House of Life* (1871) called 'Heart's Hope' and, standing as it does near the beginning of the sequence, it has the important function of stating what Rossetti hoped to achieve in the poetry addressed to or describing his beloved:

> Lady, I fain would tell how evermore
> Thy soul I know not from thy body, nor
> Thee from myself, neither our love from God.

In this programme, the conflict between siren and pure love disappears, not through self-suppression nor through chaste joys of marriage as Patmore celebrated them, but in a sublimation of peculiar and extreme character. The sestet of 'Heart's Hope' sets out more fully what is implied in Rossetti's ideal of love:

> Yea, in God's name, and Love's, and thine, would I
> Draw from one loving heart such evidence
> As to all hearts all things shall signify;
> Tender as dawn's first hill-fire, and intense
> As instantaneous penetrating sense,
> In Spring's birth-hour, of other Springs gone by.

The secret of man's and woman's mutual love is the secret of all things. It absorbs Time itself, Rossetti's constant preoccupation, as, with characteristic sleight of hand, he imposes images of past Springs on present experience. Birth and death, and the 'penetrating sense' of births and deaths gone by, subserve the all-inclusive experience of love. Love makes body and soul one, identifies two lovers, is of one nature with God, and this is claimed not for a generalised concept but for 'me' and 'you': 'one loving heart', Rossetti's or the lady's, can know the mystery, experience the mystic vision.

So far, the path of reconciliation. There remains the second way, a darker road on which lie the 'polluted coverts' of 'Love's Nocturn' and where the lost days of Rossetti's life lurk to confront him after death:

> Each one a murdered self, . . .
> 'I am thyself – what hast thou done to me?'
> 'And I – and I – thyself', (lo! each one saith,)
> 'And thou thyself to all eternity!'
>
> (no. LXXXVI, 1862)

This poem is more overtly confessional than most of Rossetti's poetry but there is plenty of awareness of guilt and sin in his work. All the siren poems demonstrate it and others hint at it. Many of the *House of Life* sonnets speak of regret and of a happiness that was once possible and has been missed. The interior landscape is wintry:

> Many the days that Winter keeps in store,
> Sunless throughout, or whose brief sun-glimpses
> Scarce shed the heaped snow through the naked trees
>
> (no. XXX, 'Last Fire', 1871)

It may be wild and stormy:

> . . . the tempestuous tide-gates flung apart
> Flood with wild will the hollows of thy heart,
> And thy heart rends thee, and thy body endures.
>
> (no. XLVI, 'Parted Love', 1869)

A sonnet written earlier and originally entitled 'Work and Will' strikes a similar note to 'Lost Days':

> . . . So it happeneth
> When Work and Will awake too late, to gaze
> After their life sailed by, and hold their breath.
> Ah! who shall dare to search through what sad maze
> Thenceforth their incommunicable ways
> Follow the desultory feet of Death?
>
> (no. LXV, 'Known in Vain', 1853)

The sinister element in this darkened world emerges plainly in sonnet XCVII, 'A Superscription' (1868). Writing to Miss Losh in October 1869, Rossetti commented: 'This is decidedly (painful as it is) a favourite of my own. Nothing I ever wrote was more the result of

strong feeling, as you may perhaps think retraceable in it.'[1]
The sonnet constitutes a striking example of Rossetti's
animistic imagery:

> Look in my face; my name is Might-have-been;
> I am also called No-more, Too-late, Farewell;
> Unto thine ear I hold the dead-sea shell
> Cast up thy Life's foam-fretted feet between;
> Unto thine eyes the glass where that is seen
> Which had Life's form and Love's, but by my spell
> Is now a shaken shadow intolerable,
> Of ultimate things unuttered the frail screen.
>
> Mark me, how still I am! But should there dart
> One moment through thy soul the soft surprise
> Of that winged Peace which lulls the breath of sighs –
> Then shalt thou see me smile, and turn apart
> Thy visage to mine ambush at thy heart
> Sleepless with cold commemorative eyes.

'A Superscription', like other poems in *The House of Life*,
may be related specifically to Rossetti's thwarted love
for Jane Morris but, though a love found too late fits the
pattern of regret and remorse well enough, it is not
necessarily responsible for the development of the pattern
in the first place. 'Work and Will' was written seven years
before Rossetti married Elizabeth Siddal but Rossetti
recognised its adaptability to a later emotional situation
when he changed the title to 'Known in Vain' in 1869.
He insisted that the sequence dealt with 'life representative' and not with purely personal biographical matters
and, from this point of view, the suggestions of a history
of doomed and hopeless love serve rather to illustrate a
theme than to constitute it. A man no longer young
experiences the rekindling within him of a desire for
ideal love and beauty but is sadly conscious of past
experience, of sins of omission and commission which
interpose between him and the desired image. His own
past makes fulfilment impossible. Not only the dead

---

[1] Ibid., p. 760

exert their influence but also the unappeasable 'murdered' selves who speak their reproaches.

Rossetti made one attempt to give an explicit and relatively extensive treatment to the subject of sin. 'Rose Mary' is an ambitious poem, telling a story of love, deception and death, with human weakness or wickedness providing the opportunity for evil spirits to assert control and exult in their triumph over the good. It is a complex story of the perils and disasters implicit in the pursuit of love. Rose Mary has been seduced by her lover, Sir James of Heronhaye, but their secret guilt is perhaps excused by devoted love and when the poem opens they are on the verge of marriage. Sir James is making a journey to a shrine to be absolved of sin before the wedding but he is ambushed and killed by enemies on the way. This, so it at first appears, represents a judgement on him and Rose Mary, for if she had been pure she could have saved him. The night before Sir James's journey, her mother brings her a beryl stone endowed with the special property of revealing future danger to the pure who look in it for guidance. Rose Mary, concealing her loss of maidenhood, looks but, because of her deception, she is herself deceived by what she sees. Her 'love-linked sin' has allowed evil spirits, 'Fire spirits of dread desire' who had been expelled from the stone, to re-enter and they mislead her about Sir James's danger. As a result he meets his death. In the next stage of the story, the mother finds a blood-stained packet next to the dead man's heart and when, assuming it is some love-token from Rose Mary, she opens it, she finds a lock, not of her daughter's dark hair, but of golden. It is tied round a letter in which another woman greets Sir James as her lover and arranges to meet him clandestinely at the shrine. The ardent lover of Rose Mary seeking absolution on behalf of them both for their illicit embraces was, it is now revealed, a deceiver who has wooed and won another woman. When he left on his journey, he was far

from intending to return to marry Rose Mary but instead
hoped never to see her again.

Sir James's treachery to Rose Mary constitutes the
main story and, in Rossetti's treatment, it becomes an
exemplification of his sense of the shifting frontiers of
vice and virtue. As we read the poem, our understanding
of the story changes. At first it seems that the situation is
eminently forgivable. To anticipate marriage was sin
but the lovers loved dearly, sought forgiveness of the
church, and meant to marry. The sin was scarcely sin at
all, we may think, but merely an unpruned offshoot of
virtue. Yet a heavy penalty is exacted. We seem to be
required to acknowledge that, after all, the sin was a
grievous one. Then it is revealed that Sir James was all
the time a predator, untrue and unscrupulous. He seduced
Rose Mary but did not love her. He intended to elope
with another woman and he deserved to die for his
wickedness. His face now looks like 'A mask that hung
on the gate of Hell'. In all this, the deceptive appearances
of love are well illustrated. A debasing lust can pass itself
off as an ennobling passion. The boundary between
virtue and sin in a love-relationship is easily crossed and a
hair's breadth may mark the frontier between hell and
heaven. Rose Mary, her mother and also the reader may
easily mistake a devil for an angel.

The implications of the poem do not stop there. Rose
Mary was more sinned against than sinning but her life
is blasted nevertheless, as are the lives of the innocent
girls in *The Orchard Pit* and Keith of Ewerne's bride.
There is also Jocelind, the other woman, whose letter
bespeaks a trustfulness and innocence equivalent to that
of Rose Mary herself. It is her brother who has killed Sir
James, perhaps because he suspects his designs on his
sister. Another tragedy of 'passion-woven complexities'
lies behind the major one, all stemming from the single
guilty man. At the end of the poem Rose Mary shatters
the beryl stone, displacing the evil spirits which possessed

E

it. She dies in the act and, freed from her ties with her unworthy lover, she is received as 'a true soul' into 'blessed Mary's rose-bower...Where hearts of steadfast lovers are'.

In spite of its interest, the poem is not at all satisfactory. The story is essentially one of a devil figure, a male siren, subjecting the innocent to his evil blandishments. He succeeds in tainting them but Rose Mary, in an effort beyond her usual strength, smashes the source of evil and is thereby freed of his power and purified. But the relation between Sir James and the spirits of the beryl stone is never made clear. When Rose Mary shatters the beryl she does not know that her lover has deceived her and dies in ignorance believing that she will be united with James in heaven. Rossetti makes no comment on this. We do not know what becomes of Jocelind and we can hardly make much of the disembodied voice which welcomes Rose Mary into Paradise. A strong sense of powerful forces at work and of situations big with momentous significance does, however, come through, even though the quasi-metaphysical framework which Rossetti constructs is a ramshackle affair. The best writing in the poem occurs at the opening of part three when Rose Mary awakes from the swoon into which she fell on finding that her misreading of the beryl had led to Sir James's death. 'Death and sorrow and sin and shame' produce the imagery of psychological states in which Rossetti excelled:

> All ways alike were strange to her now –
> One field bare-ridged from the spirit's plough,
> One thicket black with the cypress-bough.

Rossetti's imagination deals readily in images of heaven and hell as this survey of his moral and imaginative world has demonstrated. It is time now to enquire further into their status. Love and Beauty are the prime values which Rossetti worships. Speaking like Keats of 'the Principle of Beauty', he said that it 'draws all high-toned men to itself, whether with the aim of embodying it in art or only of attaining its enjoyment in life'.[1] Beauty, manifesting itself as an ideal to be pursued in art and life, in both compels the devotee's commitment and drives him on inexorably in search of attainment at whatever cost. The 'Lady Beauty' of the sonnet 'Soul's Beauty' (no. LXXVII, 1867) is an emblem of the artistic vision which claims the unremitting pursuit of the poet/painter Rossetti:

> This is that Lady Beauty, in whose praise
> Thy voice and hand shake still – long known to thee
> By flying hair and fluttering hem – the beat
> Following her daily of thy heart and feet,
> How passionately and irretrievably,
> In what fond flight, how many ways and days!

'I loved thee ere I loved a woman, Love', Rossetti wrote one day but he headed the line 'To Art'.[2] From the time when, in *Hand and Soul*, his soul appeared to him in the form of a woman, all that he most valued was represented by a female figure and that Beauty should be Art and Art a woman was only natural. As for Love, it is in him predominantly a response to Beauty, a desire which unites body and soul in aspiration towards ideal fulfilment. In its essence it is a power beyond all other powers which 'the heart finds fair' and it is beyond the influence of Time:

> Love's throne was not with these; but far above
> All passionate wind of welcome and farewell
> He sat in breathless bowers they dream not of.
>
> (no. 1, 'Love Enthroned', 1871)

Here is that heaven promised to true lovers in poems where faith dominates. But, quite apart from the perils, already discussed, which beset the pursuit of love and

---

[1] W. M. Rossetti, *D. G. Rossetti as Designer and Writer*, p. 56.
[2] *Works*, i, p. 378.

beauty and which may turn it into a headlong descent into hell, there are other threats to the lovers' Paradise. Time and change are among them but, dominating all, is death. Sonnet no. IV of *The House of Life* strikes the note early:

> O love, my love! if I no more should see
> Thyself, nor on the earth the shadow of thee,
> Nor image of thine eye in any spring –
> How then should sound upon Life's darkening slope
> The ground-whirl of the perished leaves of Hope,
> The wind of Death's imperishable wing?
>
> ('Lovesight', 1869)

The theme is deepened in sonnets placed later in the sequence, no. XLIII, 'Love and Hope', and XLIV, 'Cloud and Wind' (both 1871). Sonnet no. XLIII begins with celebrating an hour of love so intense that it wipes out past years of grief and unsatisfied longing:

> Those years, those tears are dead, but only they:
> Bless love and hope, true soul; for we are here.

The mood and phrasing are reminiscent of the climax of Browning's 'In a Balcony' (1858) when, facing imminent death, the lovers recognise the full reach of their love:

> Why care by what meanders we are here
> I' the centre of the labyrinth? Men have died
> Trying to find this place, which we have found.

But fear of death and what comes after death encroaches on love and hope in Rossetti's poem:

> Cling heart to heart; nor of this hour demand
> Whether in very truth, when we are dead,
> Our hearts shall wake to know Love's golden head
> Sole sunshine of the imperishable land;
> Or but discern, through night's unfeatured scope,
> Scorn-fired at length the illusive eyes of Hope.

The following sonnet, beginning 'Love, should I fear death most for you or me?', expands these lines. If the beloved dies first, he may kill himself and follow her, but if he does so he may miss her after all and they be parted eternally. Tennyson, in *In Memoriam*, had similar nightmares that Arthur Hallam might pass before him through successive stages of the life after death and he, living longer on earth, would never catch up. The sestet of Rossetti's poem then envisages the alternative, that the lover dies first and then, like the blessed damozel, he may look down helplessly on the grief of the beloved still on earth. Worse than this is yet another possibility, that death will be:

> . . . (woe is me!) a bed wherein my sleep
> Ne'er notes (as death's dear cup at last you drain)
> The hour when you too learn that all is vain
> And that Hope sows what Love shall never reap.

These poems look forward to the last sonnet of the sequence, called 'The One Hope' (1870), which Rossetti told Alice Boyd refers 'to the longing for accomplishment of individual desire after death'.[1] The poem draws on the legend of the Cumaean sibyl[2] whom Aeneas consulted before his descent to the underworld and who inscribed her prophecies on leaves which might be blown about and dispersed by the winds. In book three of *The Aeneid* the scattering of these leaves is said to be caused by even the slightest breath of wind through an open door and in book six Aeneas begs the sibyl not to entrust her words to such volatile carriers. Rossetti seems to have conflated this story with the myth of Hyacinthus, a youth loved by Apollo but accidentally killed by him. From his blood sprang a flower on whose petals is the word *a'iaî*, alas, but on the petals which Rossetti envisages there will be another word, 'the one Hope's one name . . . Not less nor more, but even that word alone'. This word could be the name of the beloved or of Love itself, 'Amulet, talisman and oracle', as it is described in the

---

[1] *Letters*, ii, p. 821.

[2] See 'Rossetti's Cumaean Oracle', by John Lindberg, *Victorian Newsletter*, Fall 1962, pp. 20–1.

sonnet 'Astarte Syriaca'. In any event it will not be what it was for the psalmist: 'they that know thy name will put their trust in thee: for thou, Lord, hast not forgotten them that seek thee', for Rossetti cannot and does not claim religious assurance.

> What of the heart of love
> That bleeds in thy breast, O Man?

he asks in 'The Cloud Confines' (1871) and can answer no more than:

> Still we say as we go –
> 'Strange to think by the way,
> Whatever there is to know,
> That shall we know one day'.

Rossetti, alike in the importance he attaches to love and in his inability to underpin it with anything but human longing, shares a situation common among his contemporaries. When old habits of thought and old modes of belief broke down under the new intellectual pressures of the nineteenth century, a great burden of responsibility fell on human love. 'Ah love, let us be true to one another', Arnold exclaims in 'Dover Beach' as he feels every other security slip from him. Browning, not given to speculative thought, grounds his faith also on love and uses his characters' capacity to respond to love as a touchstone of the quality of their souls. William Morris writes an unsuccessful and uncharacteristically emphatic verse-drama to illustrate the title he gave it, *Love is Enough*. Mrs Browning in *Aurora Leigh* slides, from a highly interesting and intelligent account of a young woman's mental growth and her determination to become a poet, into a silly story whose message is that 'Art is much, but love is more.' The weakness of all such affirmations, as Rossetti acknowledges, is that they have nothing to support them. God, when such a presence is admitted in these poems, is there to guarantee human love, as in Tennyson's *In Memoriam*. The divine nature is derived from human values, rather than the other way round. Hence the over-emphasis and even slightly hysterical note that creeps in from time to time, as if saying a thing loudly enough will make it true.

Rossetti shares the situation of other reluctant un-believers or half-believers and on occasions his poetry makes this explicit. Yet he is not entirely contained by it and what is uncommon in his experience is, as before, important and rewarding to attention. For Rossetti derives a conception of mystic love from Dante and this ultim-ately gives a shape and character to his view of life and justifies his setting of his own record in a framework of life, love and death. Here we come to the point where previous lines of exploration converge, for Rossetti's vision of body and soul reconciled in mystic love and his remorseful and guilty sense of a vision betrayed both lead to – or more properly derive from – the deep impressions made upon him from early years by his knowledge of Dante and his contemporaries. Dante's world formed Rossetti's mind to an extent such that later experience fell irresistibly into patterns already imprinted on his imagination. In this lies the explanation of the apparently uncanny way in which there emerge in early work motifs which might be expected to appear only at a later date, after the events which would, on the face of it, seem likely to have produced them. The first versions of 'The Blessed Damozel' and 'The Portrait', for example, were written when Rossetti was still a boy, though the theme of lovers parted by death and longing for reunion beyond the grave might well be thought to belong naturally to the time following his wife's death in 1862. A poem written in 1853, as has already been pointed out, could be appropriated quite easily to express Rossetti's feelings twenty years later in his frustrated love affair with Jane Morris. Rossetti's imaginative world was fully formed by the time he was nineteen. It was a rich and vibrant world and in the next few years poems and stories came to easy birth in it. In his second productive period, beginning with his preparation of the 1870 volume, the colour is darker and some elements loom larger than they did earlier but the world is the same world and the old paradigms still apply. The importance of Dante, early and late, is a matter to be considered in the next chapter.

5

The importance of Dante

THE influence of Dante and Dante's contemporaries on Rossetti is generally recognised but how deeply it permeates his mind and how extensive its implications are is not so commonly understood. Graham Hough glances at the subject in his book *The Last Romantics* when he comments on Rossetti's youthful translations of Dante's *Vita Nuova* and other Italian poetry: 'It would be hard to overrate the effect of these translations, made when he was very young, on Rossetti's sensibility. They must of course have involved close study, and the feeling of these poems seems to have become a part of his mind much more than that of any other poetry.'[1] The present discussion will reinforce that conclusion as it draws into the one frame aspects of Rossetti which have been treated separately earlier in this study.

Rossetti began work on his translations in 1848, or perhaps even earlier, and published them first in 1861 in a volume called *The Early Italian Poets*. 'In relinquishing this work', he wrote in the preface to the first edition,

I feel, as it were, divided from my youth. The first associations I have are connected with my father's devoted studies which, from his own point of view, have done so much towards the general investigation of Dante's writings. Thus, in those early days, all around me partook of the influence of the great Florentine; till, from viewing it as a natural element, I also, growing older, was drawn within the circle.[2]

One of the first fruits of his conscious entry into Dante's orbit was an original poem, 'Dante at Verona', written

[1] *The Last Romantics*, p. 74
[2] *Works*, ii, p. xv.

while his mind was full of the *Vita Nuova*. It is an attractive poem with many characteristic touches, its most striking feature being the dramatic treatment of the episodes. An example is the account of the public penance exacted of the Florentine exiles:

> And as each proscript rose and stood
> From kneeling in the ashen dust
> On the shrine-steps, some magnate thrust
> A beard into the velvet hood
> Of his front colleague's gown to see
> The cinders stuck in his bare knee.

The young Rossetti's passionate involvement with Dante's feelings and his situation, as he understands it to be, makes the poem vivid and vigorous but the emphasis falls more on social and political corruption in Dante's world than on Dante's commitment to Beatrice. To this extent the poem aligns itself with the sonnet 'At the Sunrise in 1848' as one of Rossetti's rare political utterances and reflects comparatively little of his deep interest in Dante's mystic liaison with Beatrice.

The *Vita Nuova* makes its appearance in the poem, nevertheless, 'his youth's dear book' as it is there called. In the preface to his translation, Rossetti describes the *Vita Nuova* as an 'Autobiography or Autopsychology'[1] and the second word indicates at once where a large measure of its appeal lay for him. *The House of Life* is an autopsychology and much of Rossetti's work derives from the same impulse, as his imagery especially demonstrates. *The House of Life* borrows not only the general idea from the Italian but also specific details, such as the appearance of the figure of Love himself as an actor in the sequence, and the reproduction of Dante's vision of the flaming heart in sonnet III, 'Love's Testament' (1869). Themes which he found presented in a mystical dimension in the *Vita Nuova* Rossetti found also in the work of the other early Italian poets whom he translated.

[1] Ibid., p. 1.

Several of them write sonnets to interpret the appearance of the burning heart and all of them write of love. The outstanding example of their love poetry is Guido Guinizzelli's famous canzone beginning:

> Al cor gentil ripara sempre Amore
> Come a la selva augello in la verdura,

which Rossetti translated superbly. Guinizzelli's poem, with its vision of an ideal love, has echoed through the centuries and the impression it made on Rossetti can be measured by the quality of his translation and also by the way that its images enter into his mind. The precious stone of stanza two recalls the beryl of Rose Mary whose virtue also depends on purity and, as was pointed out in chapter 3, the first two lines, given above, evoke, perhaps even inspire, Rossetti's prime image for interior experience:

> Within the gentle heart Love shelters him
> As birds within the green shade of the grove.[1]

Guinizzelli's poem is one of the grandest expressions of the love experience of the Italian poets but there is another facet of the situation. 'It is curious', Rossetti notes in his volume of translations, 'to find these poets perpetually rating one another for the want of constancy in love'[2] and certainly this theme emerges fairly insistently from the poems he selects. Cino da Pistoia replies to reproaches made to him, with a claim that in different women he serves one ideal of beauty:

> One pleasure ever binds and looses me;
> That so, by one same Beauty lured, I still
> Delight in many women here and there.[3]

This is an idea reproduced, rather more delicately, by Rossetti in no. XXXVII of *The House of Life*, 'The Love-

---

[1] Guinizzelli's poem (and Rossetti's translation) are included in *Lyric Poetry of the Italian Renaissance* edited by Robert Lind (New Haven, 1954).
[2] *Works*, ii, p. 141.
[3] Ibid., p. 109.

Moon' (1869). Guido Cavalcanti rebukes Dante himself[1] and that reproof brings us back to the *Vita Nuova* and also takes us forward to *The Divine Comedy*.

After the death of Beatrice, so the *Vita Nuova* records, the youthful Dante was desolated but one day as he was sitting, 'filled with dolorous imaginings', he looked up 'and then perceived a young and very beautiful lady, who was gazing upon me from a window with a gaze full of pity, so that the very sum of pity appeared gathered in her'.[2] Dante grows into the habit of going to look upon this lady whenever his sorrow becomes too great to be borne and she reminds him of Beatrice and brings him some relief from his pain. 'At length, by the constant sight of this lady, mine eyes began to be gladdened overmuch with her company; through which thing many times I had much unrest, and rebuked myself as a base person: also many times I cursed the unsteadfastness of mine eyes.'[3] He now falls into a debate with himself as to whether he is justified in seeking consolation in this lady for the loss of Beatrice but, when the arguments seem evenly balanced, a vision of Beatrice appears to him and the temptation to accept comfort elsewhere is overcome: 'my heart began painfully to repent of the desire by which it had so basely let itself be possessed during so many days, contrary to the constancy of reason'.[4]

Rossetti's father devoted himself to abstruse interpretations of the meaning of Dante's works and no son of his could fail to be aware that the *Vita Nuova* is not to be taken as a literal record of biographically attested experience; but Rossetti himself could not believe that it had no foundation in life. At the heart of all true Dantesque commentary, he commented in a note, there must be an admission of 'the existence of the actual events even

[1] Ibid., p. 144.
[2] Ibid., p. 85.
[3] Ibid., p. 87.
[4] Ibid., p. 90.

where the allegorical superstructure has been raised by Dante himself'.[1] It can be said fairly confidently that what Rossetti found at a primary level in the *Vita Nuova*, and in the work of the other poets whom he translated, was an acknowledgement of a conflict within love itself. As this is most strikingly presented by Dante, it involves, on the one hand, the pure ideal represented by Beatrice, which exists in a spirit world unattainable in the everyday; and, on the other, the human need for sympathy and companionship in the here and now which may include desire for gratification of a far from ethereal kind.

When he turned to *The Divine Comedy*, he found the same situation again. In a footnote to Cavalcanti's sonnet of reproach to Dante, Rossetti refers to *Purgatorio* canto xxx and comments: 'This interesting sonnet must refer to the same period of Dante's life regarding which he has made Beatrice address him in words of noble reproach when he meets her in Eden.'[2] The passage which Rossetti has in mind is one in which Dante himself makes a close link between his great poem and the *Vita Nuova*, the title of which is recalled in the opening line. Here is Beatrice's 'noble reproach' to Dante when they meet, for the first time since her death, at the summit of the mountain of Purgatory:

> questi fu tal nella sua vita nova
> virtüalmente, ch'ogni abito destro
> fatto averebbe in lui mirabili prova.
> Ma tanto più maligno e più silvestro
> si fa'l terren col mal seme e non colto,
> quant'elli ha più di buon vigor terrestro.
> Alcun tempo il sostenni col mio volto;
> mostrando li occhi giovanetti a lui,
> meco il menava in dritta parte volto.
> Si tosto come in su la soglia fui
> di mia seconda etade e mutai vita,
> questi si tolse a me, e diessi altrui.

---

[1] Ibid., p. 89.
[2] Ibid., p. 144.

Quando di carne a spirto era salita
e bellezza e virtù cresciuta m'era,
fu' io a lui men cara e men gradita;
e volse i passi suoi per via non vera,
imagini di ben seguendo false,
che nulla promission rendono intera.
Nè l'impetrare ispirazion mi valse,
con le quali ed in sogno e altrimenti
lo rivocai; sì poco a lui ne calse!
Tanto giù cadde, che tutti argomenti
alla salute sua eran già corti,
fuor che mostrarli le perduti genti.
Per questo visitai l'uscio de' morti,
e a colui che l'ha qua su condotto
li preghi miei, piangendo, furon porti.

this man in his early life was such potentially that every right
disposition would have come to marvellous proof in him; but so
much the more noxious and wild the ground becomes, with bad
seed and untilled, as it has more good strength of soil. For a time I
sustained him with my countenance. Showing him my youthful
eyes I brought him with me, bound on the right way. As soon as I
was on the threshold of my second age and I changed life he took
himself from me and gave himself to another. When I had risen
from flesh to spirit and beauty and virtue had increased in me I was
less dear to him and less welcome and he bent his steps in a way not
true, following after false images of good which fulfil no promise;
nor did it avail me to gain inspirations for him with which both in
dream and in other ways I called him back, so little did he heed
them. He fell so low that all means for his salvation now came short
except to show him the lost people; for this I visited the threshold
of the dead and to him who has brought him up here my prayers were
offered with tears.[1]

This is a very striking passage in the poem and, as a
recent translator comments: 'Everywhere the reappearance
of Beatrice connects with Dante's experience as recorded
in the *Vita Nuova*.'[2] Rossetti recognised the connection

---

[1] *The Divine Comedy of Dante Alighieri*. Italian text with translation and
comment by John D. Sinclair (Oxford, 1971). All quotations from *The
Divine Comedy* are from this edition.
[2] *The Divine Comedy*. Translated with a commentary by Charles S.
Singleton (New Jersey, 1973).

when he quoted the opening words of the passage in his introduction of the early work: 'Questi *fù tal* nella sua vita nuova. Thus then young Dante *was*.'[1] He quotes from the same episode again in 'Dante at Verona'. 'Behold, even I, even I am Beatrice' – 'Guardaci ben! Ben son, ben son Beatrice' – the words with which the transfigured Beatrice announces herself to Dante in Purgatory are used as one of the two epigraphs of the poem and they are repeated three times in the text itself, once to recall Dante to his high fidelity to the dead Beatrice when the sympathy of another woman tempts him to accept her consolations.

How closely the patterns which he found in Italian poetry match the patterns which have been observed in his own work needs no emphasis. The conflict within love which he finds in Dante has its parallels for Rossetti as he struggles between flesh and spirit and between fidelity to a dead woman and longing for fulfilment with a new love. The shame and remorse which Dante suffers, in *Purgatorio* xxx in particular, have also their striking counterparts in Rossetti but, to complete the picture, we have to go further than to the quasi-confessional passages in the *Vita Nuova* and *The Divine Comedy*.

Of the three books of *The Divine Comedy*, Purgatory especially had claims on Rossetti's attention, for Purgatory is full of poets or talk of poets. In canto xi, Oderisi, the miniature painter, speaks of the progress of poetry from Guido Guinizzelli to Guido Cavalcanti; in canto xxiii, Dante encounters Forese Donati; in canto xxiv, Bonagiunta da Lucca speaks of the 'dolce stil novo' and of how its poets surpass the work of Jacopo da Lentini (known as 'the Notary') and Guitone d'Arezzo; in canto xxvi, Guinizzelli himself is found in the flames which burn out the sin of lust. This last meeting moves Dante greatly. Guinizzelli's name is that of:

[1] *Works*, ii, p. 2.

... il padre
mio e delli altri miei miglior che mai
rime d'amore usar dolci e leggiadre

(the father of me and of others my betters, whoever have used sweet and graceful rhymes of love).

Guinizzelli puts aside Dante's tribute to him and directs it instead to Arnaut Daniel, 'miglior fabbro del parlar materno', one who surpassed, so Guinizzelli says, all writers in the vernacular, whether of love-poetry or prose romance. Arnaut Daniel, like Guinizzelli, is also purging his sin in the flames.

All the poets named here are represented in Rossetti's volume of translations from the Italian, a fact which would combine with the references to the *Vita Nuova* to direct Rossetti's attention especially to the *Purgatorio*. It is particularly striking that even the refined poet Guinizzelli is, in Dante's judgement, tainted with lust: the poet who seeks his salvation (however defined) through love and beauty treads a dangerous road, a conclusion which Rossetti's own pursuit of 'that Lady Beauty' confirmed for him again and again.

There are several echoes of *Purgatorio* in *The House of Life*. Dante takes care, in this part of *The Divine Comedy*, to indicate time and place by elaborate astrological references and similarly Rossetti locates the action of his sonnet sequence by a phrase based on astrological terminology, the House of Life.[1] The phrase assumes, or

---

[1] Various interpretations of the title have been offered. The astrological one seems the most likely and is endorsed by William Rossetti in *D. G. Rossetti as Designer and Writer*, p. 183. Rossetti may, however, have picked up the phrase from Sir Thomas Browne's *Religio Medici* where it occurs in a passage on sleep: 'We term sleep a death, and yet it is waking that kills us and destroys those spirits that are the house of life.' Towards the end of Theodore Watts-Dunton's novel, *Aylwin*, the painter D'Arcy, who represents Rossetti, quotes from Sir Thomas Browne in a letter he writes, which suggests that Watts-Dunton knew him to be a favourite author with Rossetti. The context in which the phrase occurs could well have led the insomniac Rossetti to take special note of it.

perhaps it is truer to say that it leaves open the possibility, that just as the planets move through the different houses of the zodiac, so there may be a state before this life and another after. A second individual passage, in addition to the one in which Beatrice reproaches Dante, also bit deep into Rossetti's mind. In canto XXIII, Dante's meeting with Forese Donati takes place among the shades of the penitents who are expiating their sins of gluttony on earth:

> Nelli occhi era ciascuna oscura e cava,
> Palida nella faccia, e tanto scema,
> che dall'ossa la pelle s'informava.

(Each was dark and hollow in the eyes, pallid in face, and so wasted that the skin took shape from the bones).

These penitents live in sight of a tree (described in canto XXII)

> con pomi a odorar soavi e boni;
> e come abete in alto si digrada
> di ramo in ramo, così quello in giuso,
> cred'io perchè persona su non vada.

(with fruits that smelled sweet and good, and as a fir tapers upwards from branch to branch so it did downwards, I think so that no one should climb it).

'Chi crederebbe', Dante asks,

> che l'odor d'un pomo
> si governasse, generando brama,
> e quel d'un'acqua, non sappiendo como?

(Who, not knowing the reason, would believe that the odour of fruit and of water, by the craving it caused, would operate so?).

The sharply delineated picture of the shades in 'Willow-wood' iii (sonnet no. LI) 'that walk with hollow faces burning white' would seem to derive from this episode. These shades also hunger and, like the souls on the seventh terrace where the lustful suffer, they also burn;

> . . . Beati cui alluma
> tanto di grazia, che l'amor del gusto
> nel petto lor troppo disir non fuma,
> ensuriendo sempre quanto è giusto! (canto XXIV)

(Blessed are they who so much grace illumines that appetite does not fill their breast with the fumes of too great desire, hungering always so far as is just!)

One of Dante's last experiences in Purgatory is that of passing through the waters of Lethe. His failures and shames have just been unsparingly set before him by Beatrice but at the climax of humiliation and self-contempt he is brought through the river where his sins are forgiven and forgotten.

> What shall assuage the unforgotten pain
> And teach the unforgetful to forget?

Rossetti asks in 'The One Hope', a question to which Dante's answer is the waters of Lethe, attained by the ascent through Hell to the top of the mountain of Purgatory. The imagery of 'The One Hope' has already been related to accounts of sibylline prophecy and if Dante and the Cumaean sibyl come together in this final poem of the sequence, the fact exactly typifies Rossetti's position, his imagination seized by Dante's great vision of creation but his own inability to attain faith and his refusal, at the end of his autopsychosis, to pretend that he has done so.[1] Rossetti can only wait for fate to reveal 'Whatever there is to know'. Neither the waters of Willowwood nor the waters of the stream in 'The Stream's Secret' can exert the true Lethean power of the 'fontana salda e certa' (constant and sure fountain) in the redeemed Eden of canto xxviii. When Dante drinks, the angels sing the psalm: 'Cleanse me of sin with hyssop, that I may be purified; wash me and I shall be whiter than snow' but there is no grace capable of giving absolution in the world of Rossetti's imagination.

---

[1] The Cumaean sibyl is, in fact, present in Dante:

> cosi al vento nelle foglie levi
> si perdea la sentenza di Sibilla

> (*Paradiso* xxxiii)

(thus in the wind on the ght leaves lithe Sibyl's oracle was lost)

The deep reverberations of the images of guilt in *The House of Life* and elsewhere involve intellectual inconsistency, for in the absence of a scheme of Divine ordinances and justice there should be no need for what have been called, like Hopkins's, 'terrible sonnets'. That they are there is an indication of how deeply the roots of Rossetti's imagination strike into the Dantean world. *The Divine Comedy* presents images of judgement, founded on the experience of men and women actually known or at least strongly apprehended as individuals. The romantic lovers Paolo and Francesca are condemned to Hell,[1] the sweet poet Guinizzelli burns in purgatory: it is little wonder that a sensibility deeply imprinted with such images should nurture dark thoughts of inexpugnable guilt in a passage through the dark wood of a tangled life. The wonder is, perhaps, that it is purgatory rather than hell in which he sees himself. *The House of Life* contains two visions of hell, in nos. LXXXV and LXXXVI, 'Vain Virtues' and 'Lost Days', but, frail and desperate as it may be, Rossetti refuses in the end to abandon hope. 'Lasciate ogni speranza, voi ch'entrate' (abandon hope, all ye that enter here) are the terrible words written on the

---

[1] As might be expected, Rossetti translated Francesca's story in *Inferno*, canto v. Reminiscences of it occur elsewhere: in the patriot's description of the torments of poisoned love in 'A Last Confession':

> 'God! what is left but hell for company,
> But hell, hell, hell?' – until the name so breathed
> Whirled with hot wind and sucked you down in fire?

and in the second Beryl-song in 'Rose Mary' as the evil spirits taunt the girl after the murder of her lover:

> What dar'st thou yet for his sake,
> Who for each other did God's own Future imperil!
>   Dost dare to live
> 'Mid the pangs each hour must give?
>   Nay, rather die, –
> With him thy lover 'neath Hell's cloud-cover to fly, –
> Hopeless, yet not apart.
>   Cling heart to heart,
> And beat through the nether storm-eddying winds together?

Rossetti also painted the episode (Surtees, no. 75).

gates of Dante's Hell but, as if in defiance of them, Rossetti's journey through his own soul in his sonnet sequence leaves him still clinging at the end to 'one hope'. It is not Dante's kind of hope but, like the rest of Rossetti's assessment of his life and experience, it belongs in the context of the *Vita Nuova* and *The Divine Comedy*.

Rossetti wrote of life, love and death but what he had to say has often been dismissed as of no account since he lacked an intellectual framework to contain his ideas. An intellectual scheme, certainly, is missing but a framework does exist and it consists of these poems of Dante's so deeply infused in his whole nature. It is to them that all Rossetti's various approaches to the mystery of life should be referred. Christian symbols occur in his poetry not simply because of the piety of his mother and sisters but because Dante uses them and gives them the full weight of grave conviction. For Rossetti, therefore, they carry poetic conviction since his imaginative need for the spiritual has been accustomed to be satisfied by them. Idealisation of love derives its seriousness in the poetry from the intellectual and spiritual authority which Dante gives it. The sense of shame at gifts wasted or perverted, at betrayal of the highest good which has been perceived, is an element in the poetry which takes on the nature of a sense of sin because it is seen within the framework of Dante's judgement of those who have dishonoured God. But, complicating the situation, is Rossetti's refusal to pretend that all these images, which speak so truly for the inner life of his imagination, carry intellectual conviction as well. The world of the post-medieval sceptic, especially of one whose imagination is powerful and whose intelligence is sharp and good and the two are not in accord – this Rossetti refuses to deny.[1] A poem

---

[1] William Rossetti's memoir of his brother gives ample evidence of his sense of sin in later years and William attempts his own account of the two sides of Rossetti's mind in religious matters on pp. 378–83. He speaks of scepticism and belief, of 'negative' and 'positive' utterances.

like 'The One Hope' is a result, mingling pagan and Christian images, Dante and the nineteenth-century agnostic, the man who longs to serve Beatrice and the man who dare not trust that the life of the flesh is not all. The combination of elements in 'The One Hope' is a characteristic one and the poem makes a fitting conclusion to this sequence in which, more deliberately than anywhere else, Rossetti explored the meaning of his experience and offered a commentary not just on himself, but on life.[1]

The polar opposites of Rossetti's experience, siren and pure love, mystic vision and sensual appetite, ecstasy and sense of sin, can all be traced to the impact of Dante and Dante's world upon his imagination. But though his imagination was coloured and moulded by that powerful influence, Rossetti in his time and country could not begin to accept the intellectual premises on which Dante's poetic structures are founded. Where conscious intelligence is engaged, Rossetti, as an earlier chapter has shown, had much in common with his contemporaries. But the patterns which formed in his mind from early boyhood were unsusceptible to merely local pressures and paradise, hell and purgatory emerge through the texture of his writing time and again. When he sets himself to consider life, love and death, he is baffled to establish the significance of any of them but when, in his own words, he shuts himself in with his soul, the shapes that come eddying forth speak of beatitude and damnation and dispose themselves to re-enact versions of

---

William Rossetti's imagination is not elastic enough to enable him to enter sympathetically into his brother's mind on this subject but he presents a convincing account of the divergent tendencies.

[1] A rather amusing specimen of the way in which Dante comes readily to Rossetti's mind is found in his reply to Buchanan, *The Stealthy School of Criticism*. Assuming Dantean grandeur, Rossetti disdains to take up some of Buchanan's charges: 'to such antics as this, no more attention is possible than that which Virgil enjoined Dante to bestow on the meaner phenomena of his pilgrimage' (*Works*, i, p. 487).

Dantean scenes. His own dilemma, vividly aware of heaven and hell and with a modern man's insecurity in absolutes, leads him to his special perception of the uncertain outlines of vice and virtue. In so far as he is a psychological poet, this becomes a psychological insight of considerable penetrative power but the fear that accompanies it, that he himself may be seduced down a primrose path to the everlasting bonfire or even that one – himself – may be a devil and not know it belongs less to psychology than to Dante's theology – or, more properly, to Dante's searing imagination which etched the images of his theology on to Rossetti's impressionable mind.

The deep dichotomy which makes him both a man of his own age and a man displaced in time and country in some ways cost Rossetti dear but it gave him a unique position and it opened his poetry to some rare possibilities. His imaginative world is not extensive but it contains some remarkable prospects – looking down the vista of the soul, for example, into willowwood, or into the room where a woman burns her lover in hell-fire. 'The Blessed Damozel' is the product of a remarkable combination of gifts and influences, not least when familiarity with Dante's cosmic vision combines with personal obsession and an artist's imagination to envisage splendidly a view of space from a point outside the world:

> From the fixed place of heaven she saw
> Time like a pulse shake fierce
> Through all the worlds . . .
>
>   . . .
>
> The sun was gone now; the curled moon
> Was like a little feather
> Fluttering far down the gulf . . .

His achievement both in its rarity and its relationship to the life and work of his contemporaries is a matter worth understanding, for its neglect leaves a sad gap in our inheritance from the nineteenth century.

6

Sonnets and self-expression

'SCORN not the sonnet', Wordsworth admonished the critics of the 1820s and went on to catalogue its honours. 'The melody of this small lute gave ease to Petrarch's wound.' Tasso used it and so did Camoens. As for Dante, 'The Sonnet glittered a gay mirtle-leaf Amid the cypress with which Dante crowned His visionary brows.' For England, Wordsworth names Spenser and, of course, Milton, in words that have proved only too memorable: 'in his hand The Thing became a trumpet'. Leigh Hunt quotes Wordsworth in his long historical and critical introduction to *The Book of the Sonnet*, an anthology of English and American poems published in 1867. 'Some will think', Hunt writes, that 'we might have done better than confine ourselves to a species of composition not yet associated in the general mind with the idea of anything very marked or characteristic' and, to correct them, he calls Wordsworth as his first witness to the high character of the sonnet.[1] An anonymous writer in *The Quarterly Review* early in 1873 took *The Book of the Sonnet* as his cue for a general essay which begins: 'The Sonnet might be almost called the alphabet of the human heart, since almost every kind of emotion has been expressed, or attempted to be expressed in it'[2] and which ends with a list of 'the uses and advantages of the sonnet' and claims that it has 'permanence and power', in spite of its miniature size. By 1880, a sonnet vogue was in full swing. James Ashcroft Noble, reviewing *A Treasury of English*

[1] *The Book of the Sonnet*, edited by Leigh Hunt and S. Adams Lee (London, 1867) p. xii.
[2] *The Quarterly Review*, 134–5. 1873, pp. 186–204.

Sonnets,[1] was able to say: 'Arbitrary as is the form of the sonnet, its arbitrariness must be in accord with great expressional laws, or so many poets would not have chosen it as the vehicle for their finest fancies, their loftiest thoughts, their intensest emotions.'[2] Samuel Waddington, introducing a very serious-minded collection of *English Sonnets by Living Writers*, finds the form peculiarly suitable for the expression of religious or quasi-religious impulse: 'a tablet on which to inscribe the divine "pensées", the momentary flashes of light, clear vision and deeper insight into the sacred mysteries of the infinite world around him, that visit unbidden the inspired mind of the poet and prophet'. Rossetti in 1870 and again in 1881 gave infinite care to the writing and revising and presentation of his sonnets for *The House of Life* and he told Swinburne in 1870 that he supposed that 'on the whole' they constituted his most distinctive work: 'in that direction, if in no other, I am pretty likely to do something more in spite of other occupations'.[3] Because of Rossetti's part in it, this latter-day cult of the sonnet claims attention here for the light it may throw on the nature of Rossetti's achievement and its relation to the work of his contemporaries.

The first flowering of the sonnet in England was during the sixteenth century and the nineteenth-century editors and essayists do not fail to make an appraisal of their predecessors. The line they take indicates their position on a whole range of critical questions and has an important relation to the original work of poets of their own time. In 1890 J. A. Symonds wrote 'A Comparison of Elizabethan with Victorian Poetry' in which he spoke of the profound influence of the earlier writers on his contemporaries. As he sees this influence, the Elizabethans offered freshness, spontaneity and optimism in

[1] Edited by David M. Main (Manchester, 1880).
[2] *The Contemporary Review*, Sept. 1880, p. 471.
[3] *Letters*, ii, p. 805.

contrast to the formal and over-controlled Augustans. Nineteenth-century poets refreshed their imaginations at this source but, of course, to Symonds' mind, there can be no question of a later and more sophisticated generation recapturing the mood of the earlier 'native wood-notes wild'. Some gifts are beyond recall but, for 'taste and style', Symonds awards the superiority to his own age: 'Having lost much, we have gained at least what is implied in artistic self-control, without relapsing into the rigidity of the last century.'[1] The view of literary history which Symonds' comments imply is reflected in the observations of the anthologists and their reviewers. Noble has no hesitation in deploring the Elizabethan want of 'taste and style': 'It may be doubted if before the time of Milton we have a single sonnet which, as a sonnet and not merely as a fourteen-line poem, can be praised without implicit limitations and reserves.' From this general dismissal he exempts some sonnets of Shakespeare and he has qualified praise for Sidney whose work is vitiated by 'the conceits of his age' and who, even in his better poems, has 'occasional lapses from perfect expressional grace'. All the same, his sonnets are 'a refreshing oasis in a desert where nothing grows but sterile flowers of strained sentiment, fantastic phrase, and far-fetched imagery'. English and Italian Petrarchism are alike condemned by Waddington. A sonnet by Enzo, King of Sardinia, he concedes is 'more sensible than the large majority of Italian sonnets which generally sing the praises of some fair lady or other, in a somewhat exhaustive and extravagant fashion'. Of Sidney's *Astrophil and Stella* he comments: 'we weary of his continued laudation of the beautiful Stella'. Of special interest, because in its preparation the editor had the benefit of Rossetti's opinions and advice, is Hall Caine's anthology, *Sonnets of Three Centuries* published in 1882. Hall Caine takes a

---

[1] J. A. Symonds, *Essays Speculative and Suggestive* (3rd edition London, 1907), p. 389.

more catholic view of the sonnet than some of his immediate predecessors. He is prepared to argue 'the legitimacy and purity of the English sonnet, as against the allegation that our sonnet literature is a bastard outcome of the Italian'.[1] In Shakespeare's sonnets, he writes: 'A peculiar adaptability of language to vehicle is ... seen to establish for the Shakspearean [sic] model the character of a perfect English sonnet. The metrical structure is plainly determined by the intellectual modelling.'[2] The Shakespearean sonnet is an independent, English creation, not merely an irregular version of the Italian to which 'it bears not the remotest affinity of intellectual design'[3] but, Caine observes, the sonnet in England has of late taken a new direction, 'a return to the Petrarchian pattern, prompted, however, by other purposes, and achieving other results'.[4] The acuteness of his remarks about form does not prevent him making the familiar comments on 'taste and style': 'A wanton desire to revel in pretty conceits at any sacrifice of naturalness and to all but total disregard of fundamental emotional prompting (which had the damaging effect of drawing off attention from the subject of a poem and centering it upon the poet) was of course the besetting weakness of the Elizabethan sonnet-writers.'[5] Rossetti himself had written to Hall Caine about Donne, whom he admired, and complained of his 'provoking conceits'.[6]

A fairly large measure of agreement emerges from all these comments, on the power and value and expressiveness of the sonnet and on the immature excesses of the Elizabethans in their handling of it. Symonds' reading

[1] *Sonnets of Three Centuries* (London, 1882), p. ix.
[2] Ibid., p. xv.
[3] Ibid.
[4] Ibid., p. xx
[5] Ibid., p. 277.
[6] Hall Caine, *Recollections of Dante Gabriel Rossetti* (London, 1882), p. 195. Though Rossetti was a great student of the sonnet, he does not appear to have read widely in Elizabethan sonnet literature.

of the Elizabethan literary character in terms of freshness and spontaneity provides the background to Sir Sidney Lee's moral indignation when, a little later, his exhaustive work on Elizabethan sequences produced the revelation that much of their work was not the original production of lively but undisciplined fancy, but translated, derived, and adapted from other sources, with deliberate intent to cultivate just those effects which in the Victorian view needed forgiveness. The discovery seemed to leave the Elizabethans shorn of credit. Deprive them of their innocence, and what was left but those 'provoking conceits' for which there was no longer any excuse?

Nowadays we see the matter differently. The rhetorical patterns of the Petrarchan sonnet have been better understood and the foreign origin of many conceits or whole poems is recognised as perfectly consistent with a poetic practice which we now see as art-full, self-aware and, in a word, sophisticated. When the Elizabethans used the sonnet as a mode of self-expression, they exploited every resource known to them to achieve eloquence and ingenuity and their conceits are not excrescences detracting from 'naturalness', as Hall Caine and others saw them, but make up the very stuff of the sonnet, functioning as the means by which it makes its point or fashions its argument. 'Naturalness', so far as it means direct communication of personal feeling and experience, did not in fact come naturally to them. When their art approached self-revelation, their cultural tradition taught them, as Polonius instructed Reynaldo, by indirections to find directions out. So they made use of conventions and formulae and defined themselves through, or sometimes against, those. That they had at their disposal conventions and formulae strong enough to be used in this way was a source of great strength to them. The Victorians misunderstood and mis-estimated the Elizabethan work because they saw only that the sonnet was a medium of self-expression and they failed to recognise the nature and function of the Elizabethan conventions. They themselves suffered from the absence of anything comparable by the aid of which to structure their own work.

Writing of Mrs Browning's sonnet-sequence, *Sonnets from the Portuguese*, Patrick Cruttwell remarks that they are 'altogether too "sincere" – with the wrong sort of sincerity' and he goes on: 'They show what was lost when the medieval-Renaissance conventions were abandoned: what one then gets is the emotion, the experience, uncooked, and the result is somewhat indigestible.'[1] The metaphor is inelegant, but apt. Mrs Browning herself exposes the fallacy at the heart of the Victorian attitude to the Elizabethans and, by extension, to her own self-expressive sonnets, when she writes that Sidney 'left us in one line the completest *Ars Poetica* extant' and quotes the last line of *Astrophil and Stella* 1:

'Foole', said my Muse to me, 'looke in thy heart and write.'[2]

In this sonnet, as in others in the sequence and in passages of the *Apologie for Poetry*, Sidney is acknowledging the dilemma faced by any poet who writes knowing that the form, the ideas, the very words he uses bring a long history of previous usage with them. By 1582 the sonnet was a much-handled form in continental Europe and the problem for an English writer, arriving late in the field, was how to come to terms with what Rossetti, thinking of the nineteenth-century poet's situation, called 'the inevitable inheritance of over-experience'.[3] In an age when imitation of the classics was a school discipline, Sidney stresses that imitation of what others have done will not in itself produce a moving poem but if, to make a point, he claims that poetry lies in the heart, he knows very well that art calls for much more than personal feeling. *Astrophil and Stella* as a whole speaks against Mrs

[1] *The English Sonnet* (Writers and their Work no. 191), 1969, p. 42.
[2] Quoted by Alethea Hayter *Mrs. Browning* (London, 1962), p. 105.
[3] *Letters*, iii, p. 1041.

Browning's *ars poetica*. 'Poor Petrarch's long-deceased woes' makes a continual ground-swell and the presence of conventional themes and treatments is attested by the nineteenth-century complaints of want of 'naturalness'. Mrs Browning herself was a learned and exceedingly well-read lady with plenty of literary precedent to draw on when she wrote her own poetry, but the Victorians found in her that directness, that 'sincerity' in which the Elizabethans were wanting. Of all the sonnets in Main's *Treasury*, Noble found 'most dear and memorable of all, those nightingale melodies, those resonant heart-throbs wrought into a divine music, those ecstasies of love and grief and high aspiration, which have been left as an immortal legacy by Elizabeth Barrett Browning'. The legacy has had, in fact, only a short life. While Rossetti's achievement in *The House of Life* was always little understood and is now little known, the *Sonnets from the Portuguese* yielded too much, too quickly, and have forfeited their early fame.

Mrs Browning provides an excellent example of the contrast between Elizabethan attitudes to self-expression and convention in the sonnet and those of the Victorians. Dante Gabriel Rossetti shared common ground with his contemporaries in this as in other matters but he also drew on mental and temperamental resources which were different from theirs. A closer look at *Sonnets from the Portuguese* to see why, in spite of the poet's gifts, it has failed to survive its period will help to bring out some features of *The House of Life* which have emerged only incidentally in this study so far. Rossetti's imagery and the quality of individual sonnets have already been discussed but seeing the sequence as a whole in juxtaposition to the most celebrated of its time makes it easier to recognise the remarkable contribution which Rossetti made to the history of the sonnet and the sequence. To widen the view a little further, it will be helpful to take into account also another sequence, a much better one than Mrs Browning's and one which draws on something of the same resources as Rossetti's. Christina Rossetti's sequence, *Monna Innominata*, consists of only fourteen sonnets and is almost entirely ignored by modern criticism, but it is a fine piece of work and will help to exhibit those qualities in the sonnet and the sonnet sequence which Mrs Browning missed and both the Rossettis found.

Elizabeth Barrett and Robert Browning first met in May 1845 and were married in September 1846. Their courtship was carried on in a long series of letters exchanged almost every day and sometimes more than once a day. In July 1849 Mrs Browning gave Browning the poems which were afterwards called *Sonnets from the Portuguese* and we, who can now read both poems and letters, have available to us two sets of documents which treat the same material. The courtship as it actually took place is enacted before us day by day in the letters and the progress of the love affair is recorded in a different way in the poems. The parallels are sometimes very close. Sonnet XIV, for example:

> If thou must love me, let it be for nought
> Except for love's sake only . . .

picks up a couple of paragraphs from a letter of 12 November 1845. Sonnets XVIII and XIX concern the exchange of locks of hair and the original episode is recorded in two letters of 24 November 1845. Sonnet no. XXI echoes a letter of Browning's of 18 December, and no. XXXIII derives from the same letter in which Browning for the first time calls Elizabeth by her pet name, Ba. Sonnet XLIII refers to the flowers he often brought her and the fact which she records in a letter of 30 December that, though other flowers die in her close room, his do not. Sonnets XXIII and XXVIII also are closely linked to letters. Literature could hardly get closer to life and here in these poems, if anywhere in history, we have a poet writing with 'sincerity'. It is true that much of the

diction seems merely affected and the accumulation of
medieval and Mediterranean stage properties, cypress
trees, mandolins, minstrels, torches and so on, even
slightly ridiculous but such eccentricities need not be
destructive. Chesterton found in Mrs Browning's exuber-
ant style the vitality of an earlier age and attributed to her:

Elizabethan audacity and luxuriance, a straining after violent
metaphor. With her reappeared in poetry a certain element which
had not been present in it since the last days of Elizabethan literature,
the fusion of the most elementary human passion with something that
can only be described as wit, a certain love of quaint and sustained
similes, of parallels wildly logical, of brazen paradox and antithesis.[1]

The qualities Chesterton names are certainly to be found
in *Sonnets from the Portuguese*. For audacity and luxuriance,
for example, there is the opening of a sonnet concerning
the exchange of locks of hair between lovers:

> The soul's Rialto hath its merchandise;
> I barter curl for curl upon that mart;
> And from my poet's forehead to my heart,
> Receive this lock which outweighs argosies –
> As purply black, as erst to Pindar's eyes
> The dim purpureal tresses gloomed athwart
> The nine white Muse-brows . . . (xix)

For 'quaint and sustained simile', there is no. xxiv:

> Let the world's sharpness, like a clasping knife,
> Shut in upon itself and do no harm
> In this close hand of Love, now soft and warm;
> And let us hear no sound of human strife,
> After the click of the shutting . . .

and for wit, which really has something of the surprising
quality of Donne's, there is the idea of the therapeutic
powers of music and poetry as expressed in the remarkable
phrase 'medicated music' and its context in these lines:

> My poet, thou canst touch on all the notes
> God set between His After and Before,
> And strike up and strike off the general roar

[1] G. K. Chesterton, *Robert Browning*, 1903. Quoted by Hayter, *Mrs. Browning*,
p. 201.

Of the rushing worlds, a melody that floats
In a serene air purely. Antidotes
Of medicated music, answering for
Mankind's forlornest uses, thou canst pour
From thence into their ears. God's will devotes
Thine to such ends, and mine to wait on thine.

(XVII)

The abrupt move from cosmic harmony to the medical image and the human perspective of 'Mankind's forlornest uses', followed by the succinct summing up of the last line and a half – in some circumstances such writing would receive high praise. Even the archaisms and the stage properties might be forgiven and if some lines and even whole poems are beyond the reach of charity, every poet is allowed some lapses.

But the faults of *Sonnets from the Portuguese* are organic and comparison with the letters at points where they are closest clarifies the reason why. What the sonnets essentially lack and that the letters abundantly possess is true dramatic quality. In the letters each correspondent is keenly aware of the personality of the other and writes with an eye to the reception that his or her words will have. The recipient is clearly present before the mind's eye of the writer and the letters conduct little scenes, complete with dialogue, with the other party. The technique is something similar to that of Browning's dramatic monologues in which the presence of the auditor is so important in determining what the speaker says and the meaning to be attached to it. But all this is lost from Mrs Browning's poems though sonnets are traditionally in their way too dramatic monologues. There is plenty of dramatic appearance in *Sonnets from the Portuguese* but little of the reality. Sonnets are commonly addressed to someone, a lover or God, and the addressee of Mrs Browning's poems is particularly obtrusive. He is apostrophised: 'O, my friend', 'O princely Heart!' or dismissed 'Stand farther off, then! Go', but, invoked so often and with so much excitement, he never takes form nor acquires any personality which leaves a mark on the sonnets. If we did not know differently, we might very well believe that there was never really anybody there at all. The sonnets assume the manner of direct speech addressed to someone who is acting out an urgent, immediate situation with the speaker, but the effect is rather of somebody declaiming aloud and gesticulating melodramatically all by herself in a small retired room where, to our embarrassment, we have strayed. The false drama of *Sonnets from the Portuguese* is unfortunate in itself, especially in its devaluing of qualities which might work well in a genuinely dynamic situation. It is unfortunate too in that its presence indicates the absence of the real drama which is one of the major capabilities of the sonnet.

That real drama is most characteristically generated by inner tensions and the structure of the Italian form, in particular, contributes to this. Structural tension in the Italian form derives primarily from the relation between the unequal blocks of octave and sestet. Mrs Browning uses the form but forfeits its distinguishing strength by favouring a medial break in line eight whose effect is to bridge the gap between the two parts. She might have claimed precedent in some famous poems of Milton's but would have been foolish to make him her example. Milton's power to wield the sonnet according to his own laws is a quality *sui generis* and Mrs Browning could not emulate it. The language of her sonnets does nothing, in spite of energy and emphasis, to compensate for flaccidity of form since it does not provide for irony or ambiguity or internal strain. The expression of immediate feeling is too single-minded and transparent for cross-currents of conflicting thought and emotion to have a place there. There are one or two exceptional poems where the language becomes less clotted and more functional and a poem makes its way through alternatives and contraries and arrives at real perceptions. Sonnet no. XIV is one of

F

these and no. XLII another. The sestet of XLII has some genuine power and XIV, bringing the male lover into closer focus than anywhere else, makes a delicate point about a love relationship. But, for the most part, amid all the verbal excitement, we remain unmoved. The heart is too small an area for the sonnet as the Elizabethans well knew. Sidney, Spenser, Shakespeare and the rest explore the map of their inner lives but take care to provide a fuller background than Mrs Browning did. There is a constant awareness of other people in their poems and of circumstances against which they have to identify themselves. They create worlds whose roundness is guaranteed by inner and outer tensions, whereas Mrs Browning creates not a globe but a disc whose erratic movements may sometimes please, oftener exasperate, but very rarely satisfy. The Elizabethans used, besides, the patterning of experience derived from Petrarch and the courtly love tradition and how much of an advantage this was to them will become clearer as discussion proceeds.

In the meantime, what drama and tension may really mean in the context of the sonnet is to be seen when we turn from Mrs Browning to Christina Rossetti. At first glance it looks as though drama is the last thing which Christina Rossetti will provide, for we are leaving apparent turbulence for apparent placidity and resignation. From the over-assertive we go to the self-effacing, from Mrs Browning's adventurous vocabulary and rash images to a chaste, often monosyllabic diction and unobtrusive, often Biblical, imagery. In fact, however, Christina Rossetti's is a far more truly dramatic poetry and she exploits the tensions of the sonnet form and the sonnet sequence much more fully.

In Christina Rossetti's life there is nothing like the Browning letters to record a love affair which is translated into sonnets and the title itself, *Monna Innominata*, depersonalises the sequence.[1] 'Monna' is a contracted form

[1] The date of composition (or dates) is uncertain but it was written some

of 'Madonna' my lady, or madam, and 'innominata' means 'nameless' or 'the unnamed one'. She could have used the word 'donna' as indeed she does in her headnote to the sequence, 'donne innominate', but the transposition of sounds, 'monna'/'innom . . . a' is effective and the echo with its rather hollow ring perhaps sharpens our sense of pathos in this record of an unnamed and unrecorded lady, one of many whom history never troubles itself to name. At the head of each sonnet in the sequence, Christina Rossetti places lines from *The Divine Comedy* and Petrarch. Her intention seems to have been to relate the poems to medieval Italian writing in a general way rather than to make specific correspondences. Within that distant framework she has sought to chart the feelings of a woman in one of those unfulfilled relationships which Dante in earlier poetry and Petrarch in his *Rime* recorded from the man's point of view. The headnote emphasises the literary ancestry of the sonnets:

Beatrice, immortalised by 'altissimo poeta . . . cotante amante'; Laura, celebrated by a great though an inferior bard – have alike paid the exceptional penalty of exceptional honour, and have come down to us resplendent with charms, but (at least to my apprehension) scant of attractiveness.

These heroines of world-wide fame were preceded by a bevy of unnamed ladies, 'donne innominate', sung by a school of less conspicuous poets; and in that land and that period which gave simultaneous birth to Catholics, to Albigenses, and to Troubadours, one can imagine many a lady as sharing her lover's poetic aptitude, while the barrier between them might be one held sacred by both, yet not such as to render mutual love incompatible with mutual honour.

Had such a lady spoken for herself, the portrait left us might have appeared more tender, if less dignified, than any drawn even by a devoted friend.

---

time after 1866. In 1880 Rossetti wrote to Hall Caine: 'I will venture to say that I wish my sister's sonnet work had met with what I consider the justice due to it' and he goes on to comment on 'the unsurpassed quality (in my opinion) of her best sonnets'. He does not specify which, of much work in this form, he means (Hall Caine, *Recollections*, p. 241.)

She goes on to offer a somewhat equivocal tribute to Mrs Browning who, if she had 'only been unhappy instead of happy' might have written poems for a 'donna innominata' worthy of a high place in the great tradition.

It may be that in spite of the references to Petrarch and Dante some submerged biographical situation lies at the basis of Christina Rossetti's sequence. However that may be, the poems have a power to move which Mrs Browning's do not and here we come back to the uses of convention. Mrs Browning had broken with tradition by writing sonnets of happy love and could not cope with the burden thus laid upon her of extending the range and significance of her poems so that the reader might feel he was participating in something more than a miniature firework display. All those thousands of poems of vain love stemming from the courtly love of twelfth-century Provence do, after all, testify by their very existence that the theme of frustrated love is a fertile one. The Rossettis were in a particularly strong position to realise how much the medieval conventions could contain, for their father devoted his later life to the unfolding of concealed political meanings in Dante's works. Though the young Dante Gabriel was impatient with much of this, he confessed to Hall Caine in 1880, concerning the early Italian poets he had translated in his youth: 'I really *do* suspect that in some cases... politics were really meant where love was used as a metaphor.'[1] Hall Caine remembered such remarks when he compiled his *Sonnets of Three Centuries* for he there glances at the theory 'that the early Italian poets often used love as a metaphor where politics and scepticism were covertly involved'. Faithful to his English nineteenth-century background, however, he states the objection to this as 'robbing the poetry in question of the beauty that attaches to it from its appearance of sincerity'.[2]

[1] Hall Caine, *Recollections*, p. 202.
[2] Ibid., pp. 272–3.

Politics and scepticism do not exhaust the metaphorical meanings of courtly love. The formula can be used to express aspiration, service, disappointment, despair on many levels and of many kinds. The beloved whose favour is sought may be God or a King or fortune or a woman, the frustration experienced may be spiritual or political or emotional, or it may be the cry of an imprisoned temperament reaching out for and being denied fulfilment. If the situation is treated seriously, the conflicts can be very strong. Sidney's struggle between Love and Virtue in *Astrophil and Stella* leads him to discoveries about himself and to questioning of accepted values in his society. Petrarch experienced acutely the pull between love of the human and the divine. In *Monna Innominata* there is also tension, as personal longing is beaten back by knowledge of the impossibility of winning what is longed for, as the effort is made to transcend the limitations of this life in the expectation of fulfilment in another world, and as the coming of age sets the seal on disappointed hope. If Mrs Browning had reflected more on the history of the sonnet and sonnet sequences she might have recognised how rich in implication the Petrarchan pattern was and how thin by comparison any merely personal experience is likely to be. Sidney offered advice in *Astrophil and Stella* no. 70 which she did not take. He toys with the idea of writing joyful sonnets when Stella seems at last to be favouring him – 'Sonnets be not bound prentise to annoy' he says – but rejects it:

> Cease eager Muse, peace pen, for my sake stay,
> I give you here my hand for truth of this,
> Wise silence is best musicke unto blisse.

Two sonnets from *Monna Innominata* will illustrate the virtues of Christina Rossetti's sequence:

> 6
> Trust me, I have not earned your dear rebuke –
> I love, as you would have me, God the most;
> Would not lose Him, but you, must one be lost,

F*

Nor with Lot's wife cast back one faithless look,
Unready to forego what I forsook;
This say I, having counted up the cost,
This, though I be the feeblest of God's host,
The sorriest sheep Christ shepherds with his crook.
Yet while I love my God the most, I deem
That I can never love you over-much;
I love Him more, so let me love you too;
Yea, as I apprehend it, love is such
I cannot love you if I love not Him,
I cannot love Him if I love not you.

7

'Love me, for I love you' – and answer me,
'Love me, for I love you': so shall we stand
As happy equals in the flowering land
Of love, that knows not a dividing sea.
Love builds the house on rock and not on sand,
Love laughs what while the winds rave desperately;
And who hath found love's citadel unmanned?
And who hath held in bonds love's liberty? –
My heart's a coward though my words are brave –
We meet so seldom, yet we surely part
So often; there's a problem for your art!
Still I find comfort in his Book who saith,
Though jealousy be cruel as the grave,
And death be strong, yet love is strong as death.

These are very active sonnets, full of that characteristic drama of the sonnet which depends on progression of thought and feeling. There are some very striking turns and contrasts in these two poems. The demureness of the opening of no. 6, for example, is deceptive. It sounds like an expression merely of dutiful platitude but line five, with its balancing of 'forego' and 'forsook', alerts us to the presence of a mind at work. It is a brilliant condensing into a line of the story of Lot's wife and it is also a piece of psychological penetration. One may agree to forsake and yet when it comes to the point be unwilling to forego. Two contrary impulses strike against each other in the situation which the line describes just as, in the poem as a whole, two loves, one human and the other divine,

make their claims against each other. The opening lines
suggest that the situation is resolved beyond question
but line five raises the possibility that question may still
remain even after affirmation has been made. The next
three lines then strengthen the original position. Having
acknowledged the possibility of back-sliding, the poem
repeats with added emphasis that the commitment to
God stands and will stand in spite of human weakness.
Then the sestet produces the surprise of its 'Yet'. Lines
six to eight have seemed to admit of no qualification but
the sestet changes the basis of the understanding gained
so far.

> I love, as you would have me, God the most;
> Would lose not Him, but you, must one be lost

lines three to four declare with apparent finality. But the
sestet rejects the terms of choice. Love of God does not
exclude love of the lover but includes it. The last two
lines express the point in what has the force of a daring
paradox:

> I cannot love you if I love not Him,
> I cannot love Him if I love not you.

The relation of human love to claims of a higher order
has worried love poets in ages of faith at least from
Petrarch onwards. Spenser, in his sonnet sequence,
Amoretti, was able to say:

> So let us love, dear love, like as we ought,
> Love is the lesson which the Lord us taught

because he is writing of the Christian sacrament of
marriage; but there is a 'barrier' between Christina
Rossetti's lovers, 'one held sacred by both', and the
declaration of the sestet is, in consequence, all the more
challenging. The cavalier gallantry of Lovelace's equivalent:

> I could not love thee dear so much
> Loved I not Honour more . . .

bespeaks a shallower world of thought and feeling by comparison.

Sonnet no. 7 picks up the word 'love' which has been used ten times in the preceding sonnet, nine times in the sestet. No. 6 has justified the lovers and they can now freely and happily exchange their avowals of love. The octave expresses and rejoices in the all-conquering power of love. Though circumstances part the lovers, love overcomes division; though all things work against them, love is strong to overcome all attack. As on first impression of no. 6, the ideas of the octave may seem common-place enough. *Amor vincit omnia* was a sentiment well known to Chaucer's Prioress and we have all been told that love laughs at locksmiths. Christina Rossetti's treatment of this theme culminates in a burst of confident rhetorical questions but the sestet once more puts a different complexion on the matter. 'Unready to forego what I forsook' pointed in no. 6 to the mind's capacity to deceive itself and no. 7 has suspicion of self-deception at its root. The octave has spoken brave words but the heart has not gone with them. The evils of separation and hostile circumstance which the octave claims to transcend are, in fact, feared. The separation of the lovers is the more dominant reality than their union:

> We meet so seldom, yet we surely part
> So often . . .

The apparently simple formulation contains a logical paradox which opens up a whole vista of hope and pain. Paradox was one of the principal devices of the Petrarchan poets by which they sought to express the psychology of the emotional life: 'I freeze in fire, I burn in ice.' Christina Rossetti refurbishes the device and gives it a poignancy and truth which strike all the deeper for the quiet un-demonstrative manner of the statement.

The sonnet does not end there. The thought moves on again to another element. Divine love is invoked to allay the fears of earth but the poem does not regain the confident mood of the octave. 'Still I find comfort' is a muted claim and the long sentence which concludes with 'love is strong as death' includes within it a full measure of what stands against this hope, this comfort.

The topics of the sonnets are not remarkable – lovers parting, their first meeting, lovers' dreams – these are part of the common stock of love poetry in all ages. Some sonnets have a more distinctly Victorian tinge to them, a rather Victorian insistence on death, perhaps, and no. 12's avowal of willingness to give way to another woman in the lover's affections could easily produce a mawkish piece. There is plenty of scope for sentimentality in the subjects of the poems but the tautness of the writing, indicative of firm intellectual control, forbids it. Mrs Browning has flashes of metaphysical wit but in *Monna Innominata* the operation of a clear sharp intelligence upon passion and sentiment is evident throughout. This can be demonstrated anywhere in the sequence but the nine times repeated 'love' in the sestet of sonnet no. 6 may stand for all. The distinctions between two kinds of love and finally the love which includes both of them are conveyed with the utmost economy and simplicity of statement by the organisation of individual lines and the placing of key words.

For all their deliberate setting in an old tradition the sonnets of *Monna Innominata* are full of individuality. Whether by conscious decision, by inheritance from her Italian background, or by family influence in childhood, Christina Rossetti has recognised that the traditional situation and methods of the mediterranean love sonnet provide channels into which personal experience can run full and deep. Noble remarked that the sonnet form must be 'in accord with great expressional laws' or so many poets would not have chosen it. There is a case for adding that the conventional patterning of material is also in accord with great expressional laws. Christina Rossetti works within them and achieves a tremendous feat of expression in what is essentially a modern idiom in spite of the antique formula. Mrs Browning trusts to her own more assertive gifts and above all to her 'sincerity', the literal truth to immediate experience of what she records, and her poems carry no ballast. They have already sunk and left very few traces.

When with this background we return to *The House of Life*, the most immediately striking feature may be its width of scope. *Monna Innominata* and *Sonnets from the Portuguese* are love poems but *The House of Life* includes in its second part sonnets on art, on poetry, on the way of the world, and on such themes as death and memory. The sonnets of part one are certainly about love but the title is a generalising one, 'Youth and Change', which matches the title of the more overtly philosophising part two, 'Change and Fate'. The two parts of *The House of Life* face each other rather like the two panels of a diptych, with part two relating the themes and occupations of part one to a wider landscape than appears in part one itself. Richard Stein has observed that when Rossetti paints he commonly uses diptychs and triptychs for 'themes of great personal significance' (for example his treatment of the Paolo and Francesca story and the two-part design of the pictorial version of 'The Blessed Damozel').[1] *The House of Life* reflects this tendency.

Rossetti intended, he said, 'to put in action a complete dramatis personae of the soul' and it is possible that Mrs Browning herself helped to form this intention. In *Aurora Leigh*, a poem which impressed Rossetti,[2] she

---

[1] *The Ritual of Interpretation* (Cambridge, Mass., and London, 1975), p. 173. The paintings are Surtees, nos. 75 and 244.

[2] Rossetti greatly admired Mrs Browning when he was young. Later he had reservations. In a letter of 3 December 1875, he criticises a poem of Christina Rossetti's as 'just a little echo-ish of the Barrett-Browning style', and finds in another 'a real taint, to some extent, of modern vicious style derived from the same source – what might be called a falsetto muscularity' (*Letters*, iii, p. 1380).

wrote of the way old theatrical properties had been abandoned, such as the mask, the buskin and the mouth-piece, and she continued:

> . . . concluding, which is clear,
> The growing drama has outgrown such toys
> Of simulated stature, face, and speech,
> It also peradventure may outgrow
> The simulation of the painted scene,
> Boards, actors, prompters, gaslight, and costume,
> And take for a worthier stage the soul itself,
> Its shifting fancies and celestial lights,
> With all its grand orchestral silences
> To keep the pauses of its rhythmic sounds.
>
> (Book v)

There are other reminiscences of Mrs Browning in *The House of Life*. Buchanan, with his usual capacity for seeing a half-truth about Rossetti, observed this when he wrote that Rossetti's sonnets had been 'largely moulded and inspired by Mrs Browning' and invited the reader to compare the two sequences. The comparison shows a common material of intimate experience and a choice of some similar episodes, the receipt of letters from the beloved, for example. Both poets share the same desire to give weight to their sonnets by rich and sonorous language and especially by resonant last lines and neither of them commands the easy, almost colloquial, movement and expression of Christina Rossetti. But the treatment of the material and the effect of the language are very differ-ent in *The House of Life* from what they are in *Sonnets from the Portuguese*.

The early sonnets of *The House of Life* set the distinctive tone of the love poems in the sequence. Whereas Christina Rossetti begins with characteristic directness, 'Come back to me, who wait and watch for you', and Mrs Browning adduces Theocritus and 'a mystic Shape' to explain how she was awakened from moribund life to love, Rossetti introduces us to abstract presences, truth, hope, fame, youth, life, each presented with a single, vivid detail. Sonnet no. II describes the birth and growth of love as a mysterious process by which the lovers who gave love birth prepare in this life to be reborn of love in the hereafter. In sonnet no. IV the lady herself is addressed for the first time but the figure of Love retains the quality of religious mystery. The joy of Mrs Browning in her happy love and the pent-up passion of Christina Rossetti's nameless lady have nothing of this hierophantic fervour. Within the frame thus established there is included an unashamed sensuality, for it is the essence of Rossetti's ideal that sexual love partakes of the nature of a sacrament, an outward and visible sign of an inward and spiritual grace and a means of communion with the supreme love. The kind of tensions that pull against this ideal have already been described. The sequence dramatises the whole situation and episodes of personal experience, whose outlines we can fragmentarily trace in the poems, are reshaped and interpreted to form part of the reading of love-experience which the sonnets compose. The value of such episodes is not as biographical evidence but as pieces of the pattern which Rossetti has shaped: the poems constitute an interpretation of a life, not a biographical record. The love poems in *The House of Life* are personal to the extent that all love poetry must be so, by definition, but they are also impersonal in the sense that their significance is not restricted to two individuals or one. The life involved in these poems, Rossetti said, was 'life representative'[1] and what is at issue in part one is the status of the experience of passionate love in any man's or woman's life. This theme is dramatised by selected episodes drawn more or less from Rossetti's own experience but with no commitment to literal transcription. The approach is crucially different

---

[1] The phrase occurs in a note in the Fitzwilliam manuscripts. The life involved in the sequence, Rossetti wrote, would be 'life representative, as associated with love and death, with aspiration and foreboding, or with ideal art and beauty'.

from Mrs Browning's and in itself promises a higher degree of artistic control. As for the relation of Rossetti's materials and his treatment of them to sonnet tradition, his sonnets have a full measure of the tensions characteristic of the sonnet form itself and of the sonnet sequence. His belief in love as a mystic experience has to stand as best it can against a background of actual and anticipated loss through death and of separation from a soul-mate found too late. Remorse, regret, and the anguish of deprivation figure largely in the 'story'. The frustrated love situation which serves as the paradigm of medieval and renaissance love poetry is still there, together with the vocabulary of worship and service, underlying and organising the experience of the modern man.

The intense mystic significance attached to love and to the woman comes to Rossetti directly from Dante and the poets of his circle whom Rossetti translated but in the new setting the idea is subjected to immense pressure. The eternity of God dominates the medieval experience but, to the nineteenth-century Rossetti, the all-pervasive element of experience is temporal change. In time, old love changes to new, joy changes to frustration, youth changes to middle-age, hope changes to disillusion, pride of youth changes to the guilt of lost days and the bitterness of 'might-have-been'. If the two parts of *The House of Life* face each other like the two panels of a diptych, the Italian sonnet form itself provides an alternative image. Rossetti almost always observed a strict division between the octave and sestet of his sonnets, the sestet invariably opening out some aspect of the octave and in doing so making a comment on the original statement. Hall Caine described the effect as a flow and ebb of thought[1] but perhaps it might be better described as a

---

[1] *Sonnets of Three Centuries*, p. xx. The image of the wave originated in a sonnet by Theodore Watts (-Dunton), called 'The Sonnet's Voice (a metrical lesson by the sea shore)'. As a description of the nineteenth-century Petrarchan sonnet it became very popular and was elaborated

flow of feeling and an ebb of thought. Part one and part two then stand in relation to each other as the two parts of individual sonnets do: part one representing the flow of feeling in the emotional life during youth and middle-age and part two, with its commentary on life and art and its annotation of part one, representing the ebb which follows as comment and reflection replace the urgent responses to love which part one records. The introductory sonnet to the whole sequence offers yet another image, that of a coin with its two faces, one which 'reveals the soul' and the other which denotes 'to what Power 'tis due'. The alternative 'powers' as Rossetti names them are life, love and death. Love reigns in part one but in part two the familiar ambivalences make their appearance. Contraries melt into each other and whether the spell that lures means life or death poses as threatening a question as in *The Orchard Pit* or the early poem 'The Card Dealer'.

The ironies and ambiguities in *The House of Life* are not so much verbal as structural. Christina Rossetti, working on a much smaller scale, charged each sonnet and often each line with tension but the major stresses in Rossetti's sequence are found in the pull of sonnets against each other, no. I, for example, with its confident vision of love enthroned, against no. CI with its frail grasp of 'the one hope'. Even no. XIX, 'Silent Noon', has its doubt-ridden counterpart in XCVIII 'He and I', a moving poem which voices the mood in which all things, even those which have been prized as most precious, seem to be revealed as worthless and delusory. 'He' comes into the lovers' field and sees it 'all so drear' and, where, in XIX, 'the pasture gleams and glooms 'Neath billowing skies that scatter and amass' in XCVIII 'he' finds a 'lifeless' scene. 'He' and 'I' merge at the end of the poem as do life and death in no. C.

upon by William Sharp in the introduction to his anthology, *Sonnets of this Century* (1886). Theodore Watts says, in his *Encyclopaedia Britannica* article on the sonnet, that Rossetti accepted 'the wave theory'.

Both Christina Rossetti and Dante Gabriel concentrate a good deal of meaning into their sonnets but whereas she deals in taut economy, he developed a heavily-loaded, complex style. It is easy to read both of them superficially and fail to see how much energy is compressed within their sonnets, requiring the reader's full attention for it to be released. Christina Rossetti asks for an alert intelligence to weigh her paradoxes and note the precise placing of her words. Rossetti asks for another kind of mental activity. To read him well, the reader needs to concentrate his inward eye in a prolonged gaze of introspection, recognising forms, events, sensations deep within the inner mind. The imagery, already discussed, is the principal means by which Rossetti renders this experience possible. It is a nineteenth-century creation, a new and powerful replacement of that vocabulary of conceits and images which Petrarch bequeathed to contemporaries and successors, thereby enabling them to express themselves more intimately than ever before. *The House of Life* with its introspection and its use of the old pattern of frustrated love is in the spirit of the medieval and renaissance poems though the heart and mind which are unlocked are those of a modern man subject to all the influences of a very different society.

Rossetti, in fact, has reinterpreted the sonnet sequence. He fills the old moulds with a new rhetoric and an awareness of the processes of consciousness which has been nourished by the Romantics and strengthened by the analytic habits of a scientific age. The attitude to love of poets from Dante and Petrarch to Spenser and Sidney reflected their beliefs about the nature of life and death but none of them used the sonnet sequence for a deliberately structured confession of the findings of a lifetime, as Rossetti did. Yet in developing the self-expressive character of the sequence further than they, he was drawing out potentiality, not distorting the form. Even when *The House of Life* seems to be least traditional, it remains still within the old framework and the antique formula of unfulfilment and tension proves capable of containing the personal pressures produced by nineteenth-century doubt as it did the aspirations of earlier ages.

When Browning was asked by an admirer which of his works a beginner should read first, he replied '*The Ring and the Book* of course'. It was a sensible answer though probably few have ever taken the advice. This major work sets all the smaller pieces in proportion by showing the scale against which they are to be measured. The long poem makes it clear that the men and women, the *dramatis personae* of Browning's shorter poems, are not merely a collection of cleverly observed curiosities but case-histories of souls to be treated ultimately with the seriousness which the Pope brings to bear on Guido and Giuseppe and Pompilia. Something similar might be said of Rossetti's major work, *The House of Life*. In these sonnets are brought together the themes of the other works, here stands a complete range of the patterns into which Rossetti's imagination falls. Here preside turn by turn, face by face, the double faces of life, love and death, which appear in other poems. Other work is deepened and enlarged by reference to *The House of Life* just as other poems of Browning's are, by reference to *The Ring and the Book*. Yet it would hardly be sensible to recommend someone to read Rossetti's sonnets first, even as an ideal programme. Rossetti needs to be approached by easier stages, through an interest in 'A Last Confession', say, or 'Jenny' or 'The Blessed Damozel'. Appreciation of *The House of Life* as a whole is probably the last reward of patient sympathy in tracing Rossetti's footsteps into that strange and secret grove where the spring of his imagination lay. The grove and the path that leads to it are a fascinating territory, worth finding, worth retreading. To know them is to extend by some degree the boundary of the world.

7
Matters of temperament

ANY account of Pre-Raphaelitism, in art or in literature, must recognise the paradoxes implicit in its doctrine and practice. A major example, central in consideration of the poetry, was noted in the introductory chapter and now, at the end of this study, another, different in kind but also revealing, presses into notice. It is this: that of all the poets who were influenced by them or adopted one or more of the Pre-Raphaelite ideas, only two, the Rossettis, found through their means the complete and natural language of the soul. To claim this is to raise at once the question of the status of William Morris as a Pre-Raphaelite poet, a question which can appropriately be taken up here because the answer to it will illuminate both Morris himself and Rossetti and will have a bearing on the whole discussion undertaken in this book.

Of the three central figures in the history of Pre-Raphaelite poetry, Rossetti, Morris and Christina Rossetti, Christina Rossetti may be said to have been the least discomfited by the circumstance of being born when and where she was. Morris as a young man pledged himself to a 'Crusade and Holy Warfare against the Age' and, though Rossetti reigned as a king among his friends for many years, there was always something alien in him which others, if not he, were aware of. Christina Rossetti, living in the family home and never leaving it, devoted to her mother and nourishing with ever more intensity her deeply conscientious Anglican piety, followed her own way, took her own decisions, engaged in no battles except with herself. All this was far from making her insipid and the most striking feature of some of her best poems is the powerful nature of the dramatic conflicts which the quiet tones convey. On the face of it, Christina Rossetti is an utterly different poetic personality from her brother but closer reading suggests that this is a misleading impression and that there are greater affinities of temperament and technique between them than might be supposed. William Morris, on the other hand, is temperamentally very different from either and the working of the Pre-Raphaelite ferment in him, as poet, produces another kind of situation altogether from that of the Rossettis. To clarify this point it will be useful to draw into discussion briefly a group of Christina Rossetti's poems which have not so far been mentioned, before going on to take a rather longer look at Morris and the relation of his career to topics which have arisen in the course of this book.

In 'The Prince's Progress', 'Sleep at Sea', 'An Apple Gathering' and 'The Convent Threshold' Christina Rossetti is treating, though in a different key, themes lying close to subjects which evoke strong imaginative response also from her brother. Each of these four poems stresses the inexorability of time. 'Too late, too late' is the recurrent theme of the concluding episode of 'The Prince's Progress' and, through a different set of images, 'Sleep at Sea' tells a similar story of time allowed to slip by till a situation becomes irreclaimable. Rossetti and his sister come together in their strong, common, sense of irredeemable moments, opportunities lost, wrong choices made, their common sensitivity to the pressure bearing ineluctably upon consciousnesses which are imaginatively alive to the moment by moment choice between heaven and hell, damnation and salvation. Time matters greatly in 'An Apple Gathering' though the point is rather different. The girl in the poem has anticipated due time and so lost what should have been the proper fulfilment. The image is of an apple harvest. The girl adorned herself with the blossom to please her lover but then, when apples should have been ripe for picking, her tree bore no fruit and the lover deserts her for the girl who has her basket full. There is no going back in time and the fatal choice has inexorable consequences. The immediate reference of 'An Apple Gathering' is to sexual conduct but, as in many of Rossetti's poems of which the same is true, the chords touched are capable of echoing more widely. 'The Honeysuckle' is one such poem of Rossetti's and, using the same image in much the same spirit as 'An Apple-Gathering', so is sonnet LXXXII of *The House of Life*, called 'Hoarded Joy' (1870). Christina Rossetti, like her brother, can find in a simple image a tissue of themes. In her poems, as in his, there is a dominating pattern and the elements are in many essentials common to both – choice and its consequences, the implacability of time and its foreclosure in death, failure, remorse, frustration. The imaginative, temperamental pattern is not supported for Rossetti by a formal system of belief. For Christina Rossetti it was and it may be that the matching of her assent to Anglican theology with her Rossettian imagination and temperamental inheritance gave her the capacity for the hard-edged irony and deceptive simplicities of statement which are so notable features of her work.

'The Convent Threshold' also invites comparison with Rossetti. It is a more dramatic poem than the others, more sensational. The cool, controlled ironies so effective elsewhere have been abandoned here for a much more hectic mode of expression. That the same pattern of ideas emerges again in this very different style is evidence of how deeply lodged in Christina Rossetti's psyche they are. The poem makes up a pair with Rossetti's 'The Blessed Damozel' and it is reminiscent also of Tennyson's 'Maud'. The blood of father and brother lies between the woman of 'The Convent Threshold' and her lover as it does between the lovers in 'Maud'. The hero of

Tennyson's poem seeks to assuage the pain of guilt and frustration by fervent participation in a patriotic war but the heroine of 'The Convent Threshold' seeks instead purification from crimes of passion through renunciation of the world and mortification of the flesh. Instead of denouncing social injustice and corruption, evils held to explain and in part to excuse the blood-shedding in 'Maud', Christina Rossetti's heroine treats the world and its joys as infinitely desirable and yet to be rejected with whatever pain at the sundering. The poem is addressed to the lover, exhorting him to renounce the world as she is in the process of renouncing it but what he is to give up is presented in anything but sour terms. Nothing in the poem is more striking than the picture of the worldly life which the girl paints:

> You looking earthward, what see you?
> Milk-white, wine-flushed among the vines,
> Up and down leaping, to and fro,
> Most glad, most full, made strong with wines,
> Blooming as peaches pearled with dew,
> Their golden windy hair afloat,
> Love-music warbling in their throat,
> Young men and women come and go.

The first line of the passage looks like an introduction to a disparaging account of the world but what follows is full of sensuous beauty and vitality. Similarly her question 'Is this a time' takes a form whose sheer, unexpected loveliness is breath-taking:

> Is this a time for smile and sigh,
> For songs among the secret trees
> Where sudden blue birds nest and sport?

The girl of the poem is only at the convent's threshold and the poem is powerfully dramatic in its presentation of the situation in which her will impels her within its walls and the natural instincts of youth draw her to the life outside. As in other poems of this group, the stress on time is urgent:

> You linger, yet the time is short:
>
>   ...
>
> The time is short, and yet you stay:
> To-day, while it is called to-day,
> Kneel, wrestle, knock, do violence, pray;
> To-day is short, to-morrow nigh:
> Why will you die? why will you die?

Tennyson's young man determined to 'do violence' in order to expiate violence but what is urged on the lover in 'The Convent Threshold' is of a different order, exemplified by the struggle the girl is enduring to purge herself of the longings of the flesh:

> ... all night long I dreamed of you:
> I woke and prayed against my will,
> Then slept to dream of you again.
> At length I rose and knelt and prayed.
> I cannot write the words I said,
> My words were slow, my tears were few;
> But through the dark my silence spoke
> Like thunder. When this morning broke,
> My face was pinched, my hair was grey,
> And frozen blood was on the sill
> Where stifling in my struggle I lay.

If the poem is a spiritualised version of 'Maud', the same may be said of its relation to 'The Blessed Damozel'. Christina Rossetti's heroine like her predecessor anticipates her loneliness in heaven if her lover should fail to come:

> How should I rest in Paradise,
> Or sit on steps of heaven alone?
>
>   ...
>
> Should I not turn with yearning eyes,
> Turn earthwards with a pitiful pang?

But the innocent anticipation of eventual reunion with which Rossetti's damozel comforts herself is replaced in his sister's poem by a vivid awareness of the spiritual struggle to be undertaken first:

> Oh save me from a pang in heaven!
> By all the gifts we took and gave,
> Repent, repent, and be forgiven.
> This life is long, but yet it ends;
> Repent and purge your soul and save.[1]

With its fervour and its clearly recognisable pattern of penitence, mortification and hope of redemption, 'The Convent Threshold' is the sort of poem which those who take exception to 'The Blessed Damozel' are likely to think a more suitable treatment of the situation. Yet the very great stress on human passion in Christina Rossetti's poem should not be overlooked. Love is strong in the girl's dreams and death a dreadful thing. She dreams that she is dead and that 'like lead' she

> Crushed downwards through the sodden earth.

When the spiritual victory shall have been gained, she promises her lover, they will be reunited in Paradise:

> There we shall meet as once we met,
> And love with old familiar love.

A vision of total consummation, in which sexual and

---

[1] Gerard Manley Hopkins was moved to elaborate further on this theme. He began a poem called 'A Voice from the World' in the summer of 1864 and sent it to *Macmillan's Magazine* which regularly published Christina Rossetti's work. 'A Voice from the World' was later called 'Beyond the Cloister' and both titles reflect the poem's relationship with 'The Convent Threshold'. Hopkins' central figure is the male lover, pleading for lost love and struggling against the girl's decree of renunciation. Yet he knows that his cause is hopeless and that the life of the flesh must be abjured. The poem treats a psychological conflict dramatically and is full of echoes of Browning and of other Pre-Raphaelite poetry apart from Christina Rossetti's. It has some youthful merits. The theme of lovers parted by death and/or sin and experiencing some form of communication with each other acted evidently as a powerful stimulant to the nineteenth-century imagination. A late addition to the cluster of poems it generated is Hardy's 'A Voice' of 1912. Hardy was much older than Christina Rossetti or Hopkins when he wrote this and in its maturity and, especially, the different temper of mind and character which it evinces, it makes a striking contrast to the two earlier poems. Some of the details suggest that Hardy had Rossetti's 'The Blessed Damozel' particularly in mind.

divine are united, concludes Rossetti's poem 'The Portrait' and the blessed damozel will ask in heaven:

> Thus much for him and me:–
> Only to live as once on earth
> With Love – only to be,
> As then awhile, for ever now
> Together, I and he.

The hope of loving 'with old familiar love' in 'The Convent Threshold' is not so very different from the hopes of 'The Portrait' and 'The Blessed Damozel'. What is different, of course, is Christina Rossetti's sense of spiritual conflict, the collision between human desire for the pleasures of the world and the imperative call to repudiate all these and look elsewhere. 'Sleep at Sea' is a fable of men given over to the worldly life which, although it may include love and 'pleasure for another's sake', is nevertheless blind and deluded. 'The Prince's Progress' is another account of time lost to the seductive temptations of the world and never to be regained. 'An Apple-Gathering' deals also with temptation and the abuse of time. 'The Convent Threshold', abandoning the cool, matter-of-fact manner of these poems for impassioned dramatic utterance, gives direct expression to the framework of Christian asceticism which supports them. Man tainted by sin, the blood of Christ, Son of the Father, and the blood of Abel shed by his brother, has to be cleansed and burned free of pollution by a rigorous and unrelenting discipline. The heart of the poetry is not pity but a very strong sense of the disparity between humanity in its worldly setting and the nature it is called upon to assume. The sense of this disparity is at the root of Christina Rossetti's ironic humour as well as of the painful passions of 'The Convent Threshold'.

James D. Merritt, in the introduction to his anthology *The Pre-Raphaelite Poem*, lists among the characteristics he finds in Pre-Raphaelite poetry 'The frequent use of subjects that have an innate poignancy or morbidity'.

Certainly 'The Convent Threshold' qualifies under this heading but the poignancy and morbidity are not mere gestures for the sake of melodramatic intensity. They derive from deep-seated patterns of personality, some elements of which – many perhaps – Christina Rossetti shared with her brother. Unlike him, she grasped and held them within a frame of religious belief, and when rebellious elements threatened to fall out of place, she gripped them till they hurt. Both her brothers protested at the severity she meted out to herself as a woman and her poetry has toughness as well as beauty, strong dramatic tension as well as charm. The poetry reveals a passionate nature, strongly attracted to physical beauty and to sexual love and an imagination impregnated with concepts of sin and remorse and the crises of choice which face man whose every day may be his last. Similar features in her brother's nature took a different emphasis and his poetry expresses the emotional complexities which result. His is highly individual poetry and so, no less, is hers though, as comparisons suggested above indicate, she seems often to define herself, consciously or unconsciously, against others. In *Monna Innominata* she filled in what Dante and Petrarch had left out in their love poetry, the woman's experience. In 'The Prince's Progress' she wrote what Maud might have felt, and deepened the consciousness of the blessed damozel. Colour, detail, a degree of medievalism, use of simple, ballad-like forms – all these are to be found in Christina Rossetti's poetry and by their means her imagination is able to express itself distinctly and distinctively and to produce a narrow but pure stream of creation which has scarcely yet been given its due.

The inspiration of Pre-Raphaelite ideas, argued and promoted by her brothers and their friends, helped Christina Rossetti to evolve a form of self-expression whose particular qualities and achievements still await full exploration though tribute is often paid to it in general terms. William Morris's achievement as a poet presents its own difficulties of definition. Reading Christina Rossetti properly is a matter of recognising the inflections and nuances which occur in a usually quiet, clear voice whose surface characteristics may very easily deceive the reader into underestimating her or, what amounts to the same, praising her for the wrong things. It is less easy to say what Morris requires. He was an extraordinarily prolific writer and his work ranges from medievalising ballad to political propaganda. Where does one get hold of Morris the poet? His first volume, *The Defence of Guenevere* of 1858, has claims to be the ideal Pre-Raphaelite production for the poems, many of them based on Malory and Froissart, treat their medieval subjects with that vivid dramatic realisation of a scene and situation which the Pre-Raphaelite painters sought for. Morris loved and admired Chaucer and responded to him in much the same way as Ruskin did towards early Italian painting. In his own poetry he strove to create the immediacy and reality of a scene as Chaucer conveyed it and to abjure the conventional 'varnish' of later poetic practice which may falsify or obscure clear vision. If in this he sounds like William Rossetti writing 'Mrs Holmes Grey', the parallel will hold for only a moment. Morris has added the glamour of a distant past or of legend to his prescription and, besides, he has something of his own to fuse with his material.

The measure of success he achieves in *The Defence of Guenevere* makes *The Earthly Paradise*, his next poetic undertaking, all the more surprising. In this later poetry, the sharp dramatic impact of the *Guenevere* narratives is lost and all the action seems to take place in a remote, beautifully adorned but hazy dream world. The haze and the dream are also counted as aspects of Pre-Raphaelitism by those who see Pre-Raphaelite attitudes to contemporary culture taking the form not of challenge but of retreat. Certainly *The Earthly Paradise* lays itself open to

G

this charge and Morris in the introductory poem seems to accept it. The shift of style is disconcerting. *The Defence of Guenevere* itself is non-contemporary but it implies positive criticism of contemporary life and literature. *The Earthly Paradise* dissociates itself from all contemporary interests whatever and appears to offer no more than an escape. It has been likened to tapestry and it may be called interior decoration poetry – beautifully designed and coloured but refusing to employ the full potential of the art. Hence arises the difficulty of defining Morris's poetic character.

Yet there are some features which remain constant through all changes of presentation and out of them a character emerges. It is one which contrasts quite sharply with the Rossetti character. Underlying the poetry of the two Rossettis is the same conflict, of flesh and spirit. For him it is expressed very often by the Janus face of beauty, for her it takes the traditional religious form of distrust of the world. There is a dualism in Morris's characteristic attitudes too, but it is not this one. He loves the world but, as C. S. Lewis has said, his is a pagan love with no tendency to the mystical and involving no spiritual strains.[1] 'How I love the earth, and the seasons, and weather, and all things that deal with it, and all that grows out of it' exclaims Ellen in *News from Nowhere* and her words echo throughout Morris's writing. It is not sexual passion but ardent love of the physical universe which animates his work in all its kinds, literary and non-literary. Over against this stands the spectre of death, the inescapable fact of human mortality, and from this life-death opposition comes the energy which impels the vast labours of translation and original composition which he undertook.

> Man is in love and loves what vanishes.
> What more is there to say?

[1] Lewis's very interesting essay is in *Rehabilitations*, Oxford, 1939.

Yeats asked. He admired Morris, though he was too sanguine when he called him a happy poet. There is more than one link between the two of them[1] and, as Morris might have asked Yeats's question, so a poem called 'Old Love' from *The Defence of Guenevere* volume contains lines which are Yeatsian in both thought and expression. The poem presents two old men of the Middle Ages talking over the state of the world and discussing the encroachments of the infidel on the Christian world. But, says one in his heart:

> ... 'These things are small;
> This is not small, that things outwear
> I thought were made for ever, yea, all,
> All things go soon or late' ...

'What more is there to say?' But of course Yeats and Morris were impelled to go on saying more, in pursuit of a formula which would somehow be effective in face of the ruins of time.

Both of them have a faith in the power of narrative. Yeats sought to defeat time in his poetry by transforming his life and the people he had known into the events and figures of myth. Even tragic events, when treated by art so that they are seen to fall into a perfect pattern, become joyful – 'Hamlet and Lear are gay', as he puts it. Pearse, Connolly, McBride and the rest are 'changed, changed utterly'[2] when they are taken out of the disorderliness and squalor of life and become figures of legend. Then beauty is born – if terrible, still beautiful. Morris's *Earthly Paradise* in its different way springs from much the same kind of feeling. Morris's characteristic use of the transforming power of myth and legend and archetypal narrative is different from Yeats's but it derives from the same desire to elevate experience above the

---

[1] Some of the connections are studied by Peter Faulkner in *William Morris and W. B. Yeats* (Dublin, 1962).
[2] The famous phrase quoted from 'Easter 1916' almost certainly derives from Morris. See appendix B.

treacherous shifting sands of everyday life and to find in it patterns which have satisfied the imaginative and emotional needs of humanity for many generations. There are many passages in Morris's poetry which testify to his feeling for narrative. The night wind raves as the listeners sit together when 'He Who Never Laughed Again' comes to an end:

> . . . wind and sea
> Clashed wildly in their useless agony

but the minstrel's song is unweakened and undeterred. When they have heard 'The Lovers of Gudrun', the listeners, moved to pity by the story, are stirred also to wonder

> . . . what strange thing
> Made the mere truth of what poor souls did bear
> – In vain or not in vain – so sweet to hear,
> So healing to the tangled woes of earth,
> At least for a short while . . .

At the end of 'The Death of Paris', they had been similarly conscious of the tale-teller's power to make pain a pleasure:

> Well-nigh they blamed the singer too, that he
> Must needs draw pleasure from men's misery;
> Natheless a little even they must feel
> How time and tale a long-past woe will heal,
> And make a melody of grief, and give
> Joy to the world that whoso dies shall live.

The story's power to give dignity and life to the un-ordered and death-bound experience of men is a powerful driving impulse in all Morris's work. Life-become-story may be the only form of immortality, the only earthly paradise there is, where frustrations are resolved and the wishes and troubles of the heart released.

The Defence of Guenevere is full of stories of sudden and violent death overtaking the young in the pride of life but, though it may arouse a strong response in the reader, the treatment is not sentimental. 'Sir Peter Harpdon's End' concentrates closely on the reactions of a young man as he faces captivity and sudden death and of a young woman who loves him when she is told of his fate but the dramatic form helps Morris to preserve some emotional distance. The story told by John of Castel Neuf 'Concerning Geffray Teste Noire' is not without sentiment but, set in a history of brutality and murder, it is never in danger of becoming mawkish. In this context, even a kiss is a murderous weapon:

> I saw you kissing once, like a curved sword
> That bites with all its edges, did your lips lie.

'The Haystack in the Floods' offers the most striking example of Morris's insistence that clear dramatic realisation carries its own power without need of rhetorical elaboration. Morris cuts his narrative to the bare bones in this tale of another brutal episode from the French wars. Robert and Jehane are captured by Godmar and Jehane is given an hour to make her choice between the alternatives Godmar offers her – either to become his mistress or Robert will be killed and she taken to Paris to be burned or drowned as a witch. Morris allows her no tormented questioning of the issue but instead Jehane goes to sleep, not even to dream. When she wakes, she says merely: 'I will not' and Robert is vilely butchered at her feet. The reticence of the handling is immensely effective, conveying strongly a situation in which human beings are pushed to an extremity in which there appears to be no more to say, no more even to think.

The originality of these poems lies in the whole approach. Language and treatment serve a vision of life in which it is seen, beneath the veneer of civilisation, to be composed of elemental drives, the most powerful of them harsh and unpitying. But there is a certain pride to be won from the act of facing this vision without flinching. Morris finds in these stories of Froissart and Malory the same kind of inspiration he later found in the Icelandic sagas with their tales of harsh and hostile conditions accepted and of undaunted fighting against impossible odds, when the fight is known to be hopeless.

In *The Defence of Guenevere* volume the pride is in tension with the pathos and the poems derive their energy from this. The vulnerability of humanity which cannot be protected from death even in youth and beauty and love is very evident but Morris's characters are not cowed by it. The situation in *The Earthly Paradise* is very different, for there the tragedy of mortality, in love with what must vanish, is presented without the background of warfare and struggle which gives to those who go down to inevitable death in *The Defence of Guenevere* a quality, if not of heroism, then of stubborn endurance which compels admiration. Fear of death dominates the central characters in *The Earthly Paradise* and they waste their lives in trying to shun it.

This collection of verse stories has as its outer framework the story of a quest undertaken by a group of young people of several nationalities who, sometime in the Middle Ages, set sail from Norway to escape the plague and seek for a legendary beautiful land where men will never die or grow old. They do not find it but in the end they arrive at a remote island where men have through the ages retained the language and culture of Greece. The wanderers live out the rest of their lives there, meeting their hosts every month to exchange the stories and myths of the lands with which between them they are acquainted. As individuals tell their tales, the rest listen and comment. Young when they left Norway, the wanderers have given up their lives to the pursuit of the earthly paradise and when they reach the last haven, they have experienced both the cost of the quest and also its hopelessness. The cost is to be counted in the loss of those satisfactions and achievements which come when men live out the normal course of their lives with the shadow of death only sometimes in the forefront of their consciousness. These men, obsessed by death, have lost what life might have brought them and they have failed to find immortality. The nervelessness of the basic situation accounts for the lack of energy in the poem. One element of the pride-pathos antithesis which drives the dynamic poems of *The Defence of Guenevere* is missing and the poem, though often beautiful, is also very often flaccid.

As a summary judgement of *The Earthly Paradise* this is fair but it ought not to be the last word for there are in fact complexities beneath the surface appearance of the poem which make it much more interesting than it appears to be. Many elements are at play in *The Earthly Paradise* though they tend to get lost to sight amid the voluminous swathes of the narrative. The role of the old men in their capacity as auditors is one of these. The stories of *The Earthly Paradise* have on the whole little depth of perspective but the old men who listen to them add the recognition of before and after which the stories seldom make. The early stories in particular concern simple, uncomplicated characters who are directed through a sequence of events by gods or angels; but the old men comment on them in terms of common human experience where no god's hand is seen but memory, remorse, man's inhumanity to man and longings for a better fate are the dominants. They introduce the realities from which the stories themselves are an escape and in this function they have an important part to play in the whole poem. Their role is capable of development and as this takes place development or modification occurs in other areas of the poem as well.

The tale of 'Ogier the Dane' at the end of volume ii marks the halfway point in the series of stories. The narrator is Rolf, of the wanderers' company, and the story is one of those which fired him and others, years ago, to begin on their quest for the earthly paradise. It

tells how Ogier the Dane, at the point of death, is borne
away to an unfallen world of love and beauty where he
meets many others whom the world thinks dead:

> . . . ah, how can I
> Tell of their joy as though I had been nigh?
> Suffice it that no fear of death they knew,
> That there no talk there was of false or true,
> Of right or wrong, for traitors came not there;
> That everything was bright and soft and fair,
> And yet they wearied not for any change,
> Nor unto them did constancy seem strange.
> Love knew they, but its pain they never had,
> But with each other's joy were they made glad;
> Nor were their lives wasted by hidden fire,
> Nor knew they of the unfulfilled desire
> That turns to ashes all the joys of earth,
> Nor knew they yearning love amidst the dearth
> Of kind and loving hearts to spend it on,
> Nor dreamed of discontent when all was won;
> Nor need they struggle after wealth and fame;
> Still was the calm flow of their lives the same,
> And yet, I say, they wearied not of it –

This is the dream of the earthly paradise set out in full
and Ogier, before he can enter it, has to be stripped of the
thoughts, anxieties and ambitions of the old life. He
returns once to the common world, after many years,
to fight for France in an hour of danger and then he goes
back to Avallon once more, divesting himself for the
last time of the cares and interests of mortal men.

This story strikes a new note in the collection and
introduces a theme which will recur and become impor-
tunate in later volumes. The insistence in the lines quoted,
that the heroes who dwell in Avallon do not weary of
their changeless life, does not stand quite unqualified in
the story. When the Queen of Avallon comes to fetch
Ogier back from France after his mission there has been
successfully accomplished, he takes one last look at Paris:

> He turned, and gazed upon the city grey
> Smit by the gold of that sweet morn of May;

He heard faint noises as of wakening folk
As on their heads his day of glory broke;
He heard the changing rush of the swift stream
Against the bridge-piers. All was grown a dream.

The Queen watches him as he lingers and then, with a sigh, beckons him to follow her as she steps into her timeless world. Between the two existences there is an unbridgeable gulf and Ogier as a man, it seems, feels always some pain in detaching himself from mortality. Avallon offers the fulfilment of all desires but the work and activity of the world make their appeal to him nevertheless.

Ogier's hesitation as he returns to Avallon is underlined by the wanderers in their comments on the story. The legend of the earthly paradise, they find, by whatever name it is called, has lost its power to charm them. Perhaps, the concluding poem suggests, no man has the capacity to present such a paradise aright and perhaps Rolf who told the tale injected some bitterness of experience into the telling so that it no longer seemed the compelling dream it once did. However it may be, the tale fails to touch them now. In fact, in their responses to these middle stories, the old men are reassessing their experience and making some readjustments in their outlook. In commenting on one of the tales of the previous month, 'The Watching of the Falcon', they spoke of the folly of unrealisable expectations and regretted that in their own pursuit of the impossible they had thrown away the good they might have had; but this is not to say that the old men have now achieved a positive attitude of acceptance. The possibility of contentment is faintly suggested at the end of 'The Watching of the Falcon' but described dismissively as the product of exhaustion, when hope and strength are worn out, and the poem which follows the story of 'Ogier the Dane' is no more cheerful than this. The old men's rejection of Avallon does not mean a new acceptance of life as it is. It means only the wearing out of all things, even of

> . . . the agony
> Midst which they found that they indeed must die.

The 'little mirth' which they now enjoy is such as is possible when, all hope abandoned, men wait only for death, even as the wanderers

> . . . watched the dark night hide the gloomy earth.

The link passage which introduces the first September story does, on the other hand, seem to promise some progress in their mood towards a more cheerful resignation. On a beautiful autumn day, mellow and peaceful, they are able 'such things to forget as men had best forget'. The tale which follows is described as sad but not too sad for the old men and, for the young who are sitting with them, its sweetness will make it acceptable. This is what the introduction says but the story itself, 'The Death of Paris', turns out to be one of remarkable bitterness. If it seemed that the old men were becoming reconciled to life and death, we find after all that there are to be no easy solutions to the pains of living and dying. The situation is, rather, that the dream of the earthly paradise having been dismissed, the later volumes, opening with 'The Death of Paris', focus on a possible alternative in the real world which may be thought to reconcile and harmonise all the discords of experience and they subject that to example and comment. 'The Death of Paris' gives a very sombre introduction to this new approach.

The time is the fag-end of the Trojan wars. Both sides are dispirited, overcome with war-weariness and futility. There is nothing heroic in the act when Philoctetes

> . . . slunk down to the fight,
> 'Twixt rusty helms, and shields that once were bright.

Confident and proud no longer, men simply wait for the gods to take events in hand and in a spirit of anger and frustration Philoctetes shoots one day an arrow towards Troy. As it flies, he turns away and tramps slowly back

to the Grecian camp, not knowing and not caring where
it strikes. It strikes Paris whose rape of Helen had been
the cause of the whole war and who that day had appeared
among the soldiers to rouse them with the example of
'One heart still ready to play out the play'. The fatal
moment, like the act of shooting itself, is denied any
heroic magnitude. The bleak, cold scene merely under-
lines human misery and the irony of destiny as the sun,
which had momentarily gleamed on Paris defying the
Greeks, is obscured by heavy clouds:

> Grey grew the sky, a cold sea-wind swept o'er
> The ruined plain, and the small rain drove down,
> While slowly underneath that chilling frown
> Parted the hosts; sad Troy into its gates
> Greece to its tents, and waiting on the fates.

In these opening stanzas the whole war becomes an
image of desolation. Death is casual and brutal. Hope,
heroism, purpose are all denied. The utmost exertion has
taught men only disillusion and a knowledge of their
helplessness to control their own destiny.

Paris has been a lover and love may yet prevail to force
out of life the positive value which is denied on the grey
battlefield. He returns to Oenone whom he had first
loved but he has betrayed her and she withholds the help
that would preserve his life now for the short time which
remains before Troy inevitably falls. He knows as he dies
that Helen will return to her husband and that what was
all life to him will become an episode, merely, to her:

> . . . all those years with pleasure rife
> Should be a tale 'mid Helen's coming life,
> And she and all the world would go its ways,
> 'Midst other troubles, other happy days.

At the moment of death he cries her name wildly but his
agony and his passion signify nothing:

> . . . yet the sky
> Changed not above his cast-back golden head,
> And merry was the world though he was dead.

If an earthly paradise in which the conditions of mortality are suspended has finally been rejected by the wanderers as mere illusion, yet love may create its own heaven on earth perhaps, indifferent to time, transcending the limitations of self, making men as gods. In volume ii of *The Earthly Paradise* love made Psyche immortal and love impelled Alcestis to die on behalf of Admetus and, in a triumph of self-sacrifice, to smile in death. But in 'The Death of Paris' love guarantees nothing and conquers nothing. It certainly has no power to outface time and death. The old listeners feel some resentment at the story:

> Too hard, too bitter, the dull years of life,
> Beset at best with many a care and strife,
> To bear withal Love's torment . . .

Nevertheless they note with pleasure that among the young people of the island there are signs of dawning love which promise the beginnings of new stories to be lived out in the future. Their reactions, as before, suggest the tension in the situation which Morris is facing: on the one side, the strength of the universal impulse to love, perpetually renewed throughout the generations, and the pleasurable emotions it arouses in lovers themselves and sympathetic observers; and on the other, the torment it may cause, to be an added burden in a life already sufficiently troubled. In the rest of *The Earthly Paradise* a good deal of attention is given to the exploration and testing of love with these ideas in mind. Love may be the element in life which withstands time and promises fulfilment of men's heartfelt yearnings, or it may be a snare and a destructive force; a third possibility is that fulfilment in love may be no more than a false goal, something which even when attained falls short of satisfying the hopes and longings of mankind, bringing after all, only 'discontent when all was won'.

The story which follows 'The Death of Paris', called 'The Land East of the Sun', is a long one. It tells of a man

who finds a perfect love but forfeits it until at last he is
restored to his lady after years of painful searching for
her. The story is told by one of the wanderers but it has a
frame of its own for it is presented by the narrator as the
dream of one Gregory, a seer and a poet. The tale of love
found, lost and refound is therefore held at a considerable
distance and the remoteness from actuality of its happy
ending is emphasised in the last lines:

> – Well, e'en so all the tale is said
> How twain grew one and came to bliss –
> Woe's me an idle dream it is!

The mood of the story is not the bitter disillusioned one
of 'The Death of Paris' but the precariousness of love and
the heavy price which commitment to it exacts form the
main matter of the story. And at the end, when the lovers
meet in happy embrace after long and painful parting, we
learn 'This certain thing':

> That love can n'er be satisfied.

'He Who Never Laughed Again' tells a very similar
story of a man who cannot be content with good fortune
and who seeks something further. Like the hero of 'The
Land East of the Sun', he gains entry into a hidden world
of dream-fulfilments but, again like the earlier hero, he
becomes after some time restless even there. His love
leaves him, imposing some conditions on him till her
return, but he fails to keep them and finds himself exiled
forever from his paradise. The two stories have in common an idyllic land of love and beauty and the experience
of their heroes who fail ultimately to find perfect fulfilment in either the world of dream or that of reality. Love,
certainly, is not enough, for both find love and still yearn
beyond it. 'The Land East of the Sun' does, indeed, come
to a happy ending but one dismissed by the narrator as
'an idle dream'.

The last story of all in *The Earthly Paradise* is based on
the Tannhäuser legend. As Morris handles it, it follows

the now familiar pattern of a man who finds another world of love and beauty beyond the 'real' world but loses it. The ambiguities in the story which Wagner resolved, Morris retains in full and even intensifies. The poem contains within itself the questions which have become insistent as *The Earthly Paradise* has developed, concerning the nature of an ideal world and the claims of the real one and concerning, especially, the ambiguous nature of sexual love. Whether in the end it is a redemptive force or a damning one, 'The Hill of Venus' does not decide but that it is very likely to make a hell of this life is strongly suggested by the link poem at the end of the preceding story. Among the listeners to the tale of 'Bellerophon in Lycia' is one young man who sits alone and sad and the poem comments on how men flock together in other things but

> . . . in this love that touches everyone
> Still wilt thou let each man abide alone,
> Unholpen, with his pain unnameable!

and it goes on to speculate on the reasons for this:

> Is it, perchance, lest men should come to tell
> Each unto other what a pain it is,
> How little balanced by the sullied bliss
> They win for some few minutes of their life?

At the end of 'The Hill of Venus', the young are surprised

> . . . that any tale should make love weak
> To rule the earth, all hearts to satisfy

but youth and health dispel the faint doubt that the tale has roused in them. As for the old men, they know too well what tangled and painful experiences the story images and are glad to leave as undisturbed as possible

> . . . the too rich store
> Of hapless memories . . .

The benefit of age, as by this time they have learnt to accept it, is non-involvement: they need now only look on the surface of things.

In the earlier stories of *The Earthly Paradise*, it was the narratives which were two-dimensional and the comments of the listeners which added the depth and complexity of human experience. But as the work progresses, this situation changes. The stories themselves become more complex, the characters are aware of all sorts of tensions and conflicts within themselves: the old men, on the other hand, have withdrawn themselves from experience, seeing the pains, fears and joys of their lives as past and distant from themselves. The young people of the island, who also attended the story-tellings, are brought more and more into prominence so that the commentaries offered by the linking poems come eventually from two angles: from the point of view of the old men who have lived through bitter experience and known the failure of their dreams and who now wait only for death; and from that of the young who are about to start on the same round of life and who have their hopes and illusions intact. The commentary upon life which the poem makes becomes by these means unexpectedly extensive: it includes what is implied or explicit within the stories and also what is supplied by listeners at two extremes of experience, the old and tired and the young and untried. The complicating of the material of *The Earthly Paradise* corresponds by and large to the emergence in later volumes of love as the dominant theme. Death has been the keynote earlier but by the end of volume ii the wanderers have come to accept the inevitable with some quietude:

> . . . long ago was past the agony,
> 'Midst which they found that they indeed must die;
> And now well-nigh as much their pain was past
> As though death's veil already had been cast
> Over their heads . . .

In volumes iii and iv occur the stories in which the dream of a wish-fulfilment world is tested and found wanting and along with these goes the questioning and analysis of love. The outstanding example of the later, emotionally and psychologically more complex story, and also of the treatment of the love theme is 'The Lovers of Gudrun' based on the Icelandic Laxdale saga. In this story of Bodli and Kiartan, friends and foster-brothers, their love for Gudrun becomes a 'heap of smouldering love and hate' in which the drama of guilt, remorse, despair, pain is made fully articulate. The detachment of the saga writers is replaced by Morris's full involvement in this tale of men and women caught up in a destructive passion which blasts their lives. No other story in *The Earthly Paradise* has the power of this one but the notes struck in 'The Lovers of Gudrun' are heard elsewhere in the last two volumes and the poem becomes stronger and darker as it proceeds. The mood of self-indulgence which seems to dominate the early volumes is, as has been noticed, subject to comments by the old men but the criticisms acquire greater force later when the stories themselves deal with conflict and dismay and the life–death antithesis becomes complicated by doubt about where the value of life itself resides. As it has been described so far, the poem is a self-expressive work but deviously, cumbersomely so. Stories and commentaries gradually acquire the function of images conveying the pattern of temperament and experience which underlies the whole but the diffuseness of the total poem inevitably involves dispersal and diminution of effect.

The truth of this can be illustrated by attention to the one structural element in *The Earthly Paradise* which has not yet been discussed but which produces the most powerful writing in the whole poem. When he was young, Morris's temperamental needs were met by the uncompromising treatment of the stories in *The Defence of Guenevere* volume. Translation and retelling of the Icelandic sagas followed the same lines but *The Earthly Paradise* indicates that such work was no longer adequate to contain the stresses and complexities which Morris, as he grew older, perceived. A modern man's experience cannot easily be encompassed in an archaic story, heartening and therapeutic though such stories may be. *The Earthly Paradise* evolves, consequently, a mixed form – it retains the stories but adds the quest and experience of the wanderers and the commentaries of the old men. These elements have been discussed, but even these are not enough. The poem also includes lyrics headed with the name of the month, which introduce each pair of stories to be told at that time, and in these, finally, Morris expresses himself more intimately and with less objectification than anywhere else. The poems might have been expected to consist of lyric evocations of natural sights and sounds but in fact it is the link passages which contain fuller and more detailed natural description. The use of nature in the month lyrics is symbolic rather than descriptive, for the subject of these poems is the grief of one man's life, beginning with the dread of death but concentrating increasingly on the failure of love. Mackail described the lyrics as autobiographical and they can hardly be otherwise. When they are added to *The Earthly Paradise* its design is seen to be an intricate one, narrative, comment and personal lyric continually interlacing and reordering the dominant motifs in new arrangements. The early stories celebrate life with pagan simplicity and the listeners comment with the voice of humanity caught in the trap of mortality and bitterly resenting their fate. Later stories tell of the pains and tensions of experience and the listeners divide into the old who are now spectators in the play, no longer actors in it, and the young who go eager-eyed to take up their roles. These are all undifferentiated voices but to make up the full sum Morris adds one undisguisedly personal voice and one individual record of a life damaged by the passing of time and the failing of love. One man's personal pain is in a sense only a footnote to *The Earthly Paradise*; in another it is the heart of the whole matter, the point at which all the lines of narrative and comment converge or from which they all radiate.

Two of the most striking of the month lyrics are those for January and February. Since Morris is using the old calendar in which the year begins in March, these are the concluding lyrics of the whole poem. 'January' begins with a passage of natural description deeply imbued, like Pre-Raphaelite paintings and similar passages in Rossetti's poetry, with symbolic significance. The lines evoke a relationship which has been starved of warmth and radiance and which is on the verge of total exhaustion:

> . . . this dull rainy undersky and low,
> This murky ending of a leaden day,
> That never knew the sun, this half-thawed snow,
> These tossing black boughs faint against the grey
> Of gathering night . . .

The description is not a static one for it occurs as part of a sentence recording movement. The woman is in the act of turning away from a window where she has been looking at the scene: 'From this dull rainy undersky... thou turnest, dear, away...' The poet can just make out through the dusk of the room her 'kindly smile' as she turns towards him. Then light is suddenly brought into the room plunging the scene outside the window into darkness:

> And in the sudden change our eyes meet dazed –
> O look, love, look again! the veil of doubt
> Just for one flash, past counting, then was raised!
> O eyes of heaven, as clear thy sweet soul blazed
> On mine a moment! . . .

There are quintessential Pre-Raphaelite techniques at work in producing the effect of this. The arrested movement which becomes a significant moment and into which the experience of years, it may be, rushes; the dramatic incident of the change in the light which upsets the relation between inner and outer scene and catches the woman unprepared so that her careful defensive 'kindness' momentarily slips away and they exchange one glance of real communion. As in the wave movement of a Rossetti sonnet, there is a flow and ebb pattern in Morris's poem, feeling running strongly in the first two stanzas and the last stanza making its comment as the moment ebbs away, pain returns and, with it, the necessity for patience. The final lines evoke the clouds and wind of the rainy night again, as darkness returns to the relationship after the one, fleeting, flash of illumination.

'February', the last of the poems, has no note of hope, however brief. A natural scene, landscape this time, is again the principal medium of expression. The clarity and precision with which it is treated indicate the formative influences and the idea of single days etched on the memory which, for good or ill nothing can erase, is reminiscent of Rossetti's poems on a similar theme. The events which lie behind Morris's 'February' are implied, not recorded:

> The useless hope, the useless craving pain,
> That made thy face, that lonely noontide, wet
> With more than beating of the chilly rain

– but it is all the same a dramatic impulse which gives rise to the poem. Amidst the barren desolate February world he anticipates a spring to come when a bright dawn will break on the green earth and he forebodes that even then he will see only the winter landscape:

> Thou shalt awake, and thinking of days dead,
> See nothing clear but this same dreary day,
> Of all the days that have passed o'er thine head

The irony of the renewal of the earth contrasted with man's incapacity to be reborn out of grief into new joy gives motive force to the poem. The idea is hardly original but the treatment gives a sharp edge to the pain.

Morris's way to self-expression is circuitous. His attitude to life and death are absorbed relatively simply into his telling of the stories in *The Defence of Guenevere* volume; but when love enters his experience and is found not only to be itself vulnerable to time and change but, also, by the disappointments and frustrations it brings, to extinguish the joy of life which he sought so jealously to guard, then the mixed feelings, the contrary directions in which his nature pulls, lead him to develop a form large and mixed enough to contain them. There is the power of narrative to convert men's activities into timeless myth and this casts its spell upon the hearers of *The Earthly Paradise* though it can never quite capture their assent and conquer their scepticism; and there is the individual experience, as it is lived out day by day when the future is unknown and memory of the past adds sadness to the present. Christina Rossetti accepted a traditional frame-work for her experience and was thereby made free to express herself with a fine economy. Rossetti accepted no such framework but the 'deep structure' of his imagination is much like his sister's and the patterns which emerge in his poetry are related to religious experience and have heaven and hell as their polarities. Morris, without any such frame, casts widely and even wildly for the symbols which will enable him to speak out what is in him. Only in the month lyrics does he achieve the concentrated and entirely satisfying form which a thoroughly understood and controlled group of images gives him.

Self-expression for Morris is impeded for another reason too. It was something he only partly wanted – consciously, perhaps, he did not want it at all. Not for him the urge to paint his own soul as Rossetti's Chiaro dell'Erma did. Instead he sought to turn outwards and to hearten the world with great stories and legends of the past. Yet he had imbibed and responded to the influence of Rossetti and Pre-Raphaelite ideas which combined fidelity to physical observation with intense awareness of the psychological moment. Morris was unable to deny the impulse to articulate the opposing forces within him-self and the complex structure of *The Earthly Paradise* half confesses, half conceals this urge. Christina Rossetti and her brother, in their several ways and with their different emphases, were able not infrequently to find the image which spoke 'truth' as they apprehended it but there were strong inhibitions upon the mature Morris and only on a few occasions does he allow himself to make use of the full self-expressive possibilities of Pre-Raphaelite ideology.

This returns us to the final Pre-Raphaelite paradox, formulated at the beginning of this chapter: that of all the poets who can be described as Pre-Raphaelites, for only the two Rossettis does Pre-Raphaelitism offer a complete medium of expression. The intensity of their personal vision brought together acute physical perception and penetrating introspection and in their hands Pre-Raphaelitism became the means for expressing their deepest selves. In them were combined strong impulses which in others were weak or separated or crossed by other things. The comparison with Morris brings this out sharply for he is a Pre-Raphaelite poet whose instincts were in some ways hostile to Pre-Raphaelitism. He hankered for the role of minstrel in an organic society but in ungenial times he could not escape the need to give expression to his own heart. In later poetry his personal voice is half muffled but when it sounds its accents identify themselves at once as deriving from the Pre-Raphaelite inheritance.

Pre-Raphaelitism was in essence eccentric and indivi-dualistic. It inspired many, among them the sister, with whom Rossetti had much in common, and the friend, with whom he had little. If the samplings from the work of Christina Rossetti and William Morris which have been made in this chapter are compared with the work of Rossetti studied more fully earlier, many distinctions are obvious. They developed different styles and different vocabulary. More crucially, while Rossetti shut himself within his soul and fixed his eyes on the shapes that came eddying forth, Morris could not commit himself to poetry so centred on the self and Christina Rossetti sought to subdue the demanding ego by surrender to another claim. But beyond the distinctions is the uniting fact of their 'fresh intuition' and, whatever the individual strengths and weaknesses, their best work is a major achievement of Pre-Raphaelitism. Not only because of his own accomplishment, but also because he was the initiating and dominating influence, it is a major achievement of Rossetti too.

Appendix A
Hardy and Rossetti

THAT his reading of Rossetti exerted a deep and perhaps surprising influence on Hardy has been suggested several times in the course of this study. There is direct evidence of Hardy's interest in Rossetti in his short story *An Imaginative Woman*, first published in *Pall Mall Magazine* in April 1894. The story concerns a young poet, Robert Trewe, who lives the life of a recluse and finally commits suicide as a result of 'a terrible slating' he receives in a Review – 'His poetry is rather too erotic and passionate you know for some tastes', a friend comments. There can be no doubt that Hardy had Rossetti in mind in creating Trewe (the name probably indicates a real-life counterpart) though he avoids making every detail match. One of Trewe's poems is called 'Severed Lives' which recalls sonnet XL in *The House of Life*, 'Severed Selves', and the opening lines of sonnet LV, 'Stillborn Love', are quoted in the story. As well as direct parallels, the poem contains ironies, one of them being Trewe's suicide letter in which he laments the lack of a mother or sister 'or a female friend of another sort tenderly devoted to me' who might have made it worth while his continuing to live. Rossetti himself attempted suicide though with no lack of the female sympathy of either sort which Trewe misses. Hardy seems to be making a serious judgement in what follows. The letter continues: 'I have long dreamt of such an unattainable creature, as you know; and she, this undiscoverable, elusive one, inspired my last volume; the imaginary woman alone, for, in spite of what has been said in some quarters, there is no real woman behind the title. She has continued to the last unrevealed, unmet, unwon.' This seems to be Hardy's reply to Buchanan's attack on Rossetti and to scandal-mongering of his time and since. He interprets the love poetry, 'too erotic and passionate . . . for some tastes', in terms of Rossetti's quest for the Lady Beauty whom he followed

> How passionately and irretrievably,
> In what fond flight, how many ways and days.

It is not 'fleshly' at all, but ideal.

Hardy's Rossetti, on the evidence of this story, was a very Hardy-an figure, one of those sensitive beings whom life inexorably cheats and torments: 'The large dark eyes . . . showed an unlimited capacity for misery; they looked out from beneath well-shaped brows as if they were reading the universe in the microcosm of the confronter's face, and were not altogether overjoyed at what the spectacle portended.' Holman Hunt's portrait of the young Rossetti seems to be the image behind the photograph of Trewe which Hardy describes in this passage. Photographs of Rossetti in later years show him wearing the slouched hat which Trewe also has.

I am grateful to Dr Stanley Wells for having first pointed out this story of Hardy's to me.

Appendix B
'Changed, changed utterly'

THE late prose romances of William Morris have enjoyed a revival in recent years but it is probably still true that few people read the earlier tales published in the *Oxford and Cambridge Magazine* in 1856. Yeats was a great admirer of the late romances and wrote of them that they were 'the only books I ever read slowly so that I might not come quickly to the end'. As for the earlier tales, there is a striking piece of testimony to the impression that one, at least, made on him.

In a story entitled 'A Dream', Morris tells a tale of lovers who fall into the power of a supernatural agency: they live many lives, it seems, in many guises, and from time to time, once in a hundred years it may be, they are allowed briefly to come together and recognise each other. Morris makes the most of the atmosphere created by the opening sentence: 'I dreamed once, that four men sat by the winter fire talking and telling tales in a house that the wind howled round', and as the strange story develops, it becomes doubtful even whether all these four men are alive or dead.

One of them, old Hugh, tells of witnessing a meeting between the parted lovers. He was visiting a hospital where victims of plague were lying and a woman with beautiful eyes but an ugly face and peevish temper was going from bed to bed with him. The pair come to a man who is not a victim of the plague but who has been severely wounded in an attack by robbers and the woman kneels by his bed to tend him:

'Oh Christ! As the sun went down on that dim misty day, the clouds and the thickly-packed mist cleared off, to let him shine on us, on that chamber of woes and bitter unpurifying tears; and the sunlight wrapped these two, the sick man and the ministering woman, shone on them – changed, changed utterly. Good Lord! How was I struck dumb, nay, almost blinded by that change' for the woman had become a 'wonderfully beautiful maiden' and he, 'no longer the grim, strong, wounded man, but fair, and in the first bloom of youth'.

Yeats's imagination must have been strongly engaged by this story for the phrase 'changed, changed utterly' to have made so deep an impact that he retained it and reissued it in *Easter 1916*:

> All changed, changed utterly:
> A terrible beauty is born.

Perhaps the poem owes more than a verbal echo to Morris. The transformation which takes place in 'A Dream' includes the poem's idea that glory irradiates figures who have seemed unprepossessing. The knight's wounds associate him with violence and the scene in the plague hospital with its 'woes and bitter unpurifying tears' gives a 'terrible' setting to the sudden beauty of the lovers. Perhaps even, the woman of the story, who taunts her knight with his reluctance to go to war and challenges him to spend a night in a haunted cave (this is the episode which sets in motion the whole train of events), was linked in Yeats's mind with Maud Gonne, who urged men to the action which led to the events his poem commemorates.

Index of Rossetti's Works

I VERSE

II PROSE

General Index

Q2